ILLUSTRATION NOW!
4

Ed. Julius Wiedemann

ILLUSTRATION NOW!

4

TASCHEN

Contents
Inhalt / Sommaire

Alone in the Crowd: the Illustrator Now!

by Bruno Porto

Having recently become a father to a wonderful boy, I started seeing similarities between the births of a child and an illustration, since theoretically they both may take place in solitude (as my work does) or in a noisy room full of people and machines (as Artur's birth did). If pregnancies usually start with two people (let's not get into that), no matter how present and supportive the partner may be, it is definitely carried on alone by the mother. Analogously, the labour of an illustrator has always struck me as being solitary too.

This is true not only regarding artists who strive alone in their studios but also relates to those who work in a team or partnership with other illustrators, art/creative directors, designers, editors or writers. Nevertheless, the very act of touching a tool on a surface (pencil on paper, brush on canvas, pen on tablet) to mark it is a solo action. Like the pregnant woman, the artist may be assisted by others, but ultimately is also on his or her own. As the mother-to-be follows advice from doctors, friends and Google, the artist may be art- or budget-directed, tracing a photograph, interpreting a manuscript, respecting guidelines set decades ago, or just following, for simple amusement, one line after the next.

So, whether caused by an external source or self-inflicted, the illustrator is pregnant with the illustration and will mentally deal with it alone. As he or she struggles with different ways to develop an artificial (therefore, ART) visual representation of an aspect of reality, their mind filters all the knowledge, references, personal and professional experiences it has been acquiring since that first doodle and balances it with current sets of tools, mood, deadlines, aspirations, and so on. Final or draft, it will probably go through some degree of interference from others – inker or colourist, editor or designer, printer or censor – but it could also reach its final destination undefiled.

Despite that, like babies, illustrations reflect their illustrators. Maybe not necessarily their ambitions, their best, or their personal motto, but they do display aspects of their lives: their deadlines, their bills, their network, their temper, their upbringing, their environment, their artistic choices.

Maybe as a way to balance the seclusion of the job, once the illustration is out of the house, it is rare to find an illustrator who doesn't long for contact. Every day, members of groups of enthusiasts or professional associations exchange thousands of e-messages on different aspects of the profession and blog their opinions on social networks and online directories. Promoted or entirely organised in the virtual realm, even face-to-face gatherings have now become more frequent and accessible. Sometimes a bit shy, the illustrator has been leaving his or her lair to meet peers, admirers and idols, in worldwide sketch-crawls, at comics conventions, lectures and debates, figure-drawing sessions or just for a beer. Hopefully, to get another illustration in the making.

This is why publications like the one you're reading are so important. It helps connect illustration professionals not only with other people but with their own time. To create a record of the NOW! in illustration, to foment the debate, to celebrate and reveal known and unknown talents, to allow us to grow by seeing the world through somebody else's eyes. And also for easing a little the solitude of the illustrator in a world full of images, information, sound and fury.

← Embrion, by Evgeny Kiselev,
2010, personal work; digital

Allein in der Menge: der „Illustrator Now"!

von Bruno Porto

Als ich vor Kurzem Vater eines wundervollen kleinen Jungen wurde, fiel mir die Ähnlichkeit zwischen der Geburt eines Kindes und der Entstehung einer Illustration auf. Beide können theoretisch in der Einsamkeit stattfinden (wie es bei meiner Arbeit der Fall ist) oder in einem lauten Raum voller Menschen und Maschinen (so war es bei Arturs Geburt). Zwar nimmt eine Schwangerschaft gewöhnlich mit zwei Menschen ihren Lauf (aber das wollen wir hier nicht weiter vertiefen), aber egal, wie präsent und unterstützend der Partner auch sein mag, die Schwangerschaft ist zunächst einmal Sache der Mutter allein. Entsprechend empfand ich auch die Arbeit eines Illustrators immer als etwas Eigenbrötlerisches.

Das trifft nicht nur auf solche Künstler zu, die sich allein in ihren Studios abmühen, sondern gilt auch für jene, die im Team oder gemeinsam mit anderen Illustratoren, Art oder Creative Directors, Designern, Redakteuren oder Autoren arbeiten. Dennoch bleibt der simple Vorgang, mit dem Werkzeug eine Oberfläche zu berühren (Stift auf Papier, Pinsel auf Leinwand oder Touchpen auf Tablet), um eine Linie zu ziehen, die Aktion eines Solisten. Ähnlich wie eine Schwangere kann der Künstler sich von anderen unterstützen lassen, bleibt aber letzten Endes auf sich gestellt. So wie die werdende Mutter dem Rat des Arztes, von Freunden oder gar Google folgt, kann der Künstler sich an Kunst oder Budget orientieren, eine Fotografie durchpausen, ein Manuskript interpretieren, sich an vor Jahrzehnten festgelegten Richtlinien orientieren oder einfach aus Spaß an der Freude eine Linie nach der anderen zeichnen.

Es ist also gleichgültig, ob er sich durch äußeren Anlass oder aus eigenem Antrieb an die Gestaltung macht – der Illustrator geht mit seinem Bild schwanger und setzt sich allein damit auseinander. Während er mit den verschiedenen Möglichkeiten ringt, eine künstliche (oder auch kunstvolle) visuelle Darstellung eines Aspekts der Realität zu entwickeln, filtert der Geist alles Wissen, Referenzen und Anklänge, persönliche und professionelle Erfahrungen, die er seit jenem ersten Gekritzel aufgesogen hat, und balanciert dies gegen das aktuell vorhandene Instrumentarium, Stimmung, Abgabetermine, Bestreben, Sehnsüchte usw. aus. Ob finale oder Entwurfsversion – wahrscheinlich wird sie in gewissem Maße auch noch von anderen weiter beeinflusst: von dem Inker oder Koloristen, dem Redakteur oder Designer, dem Drucker oder dem Zensor. Möglich ist aber auch, dass die Arbeit ihren Zielort rein und unverändert erreicht.

Trotzdem spiegeln Illustrationen – wie Babys – ihre Schöpfer wider. Vielleicht nicht unbedingt deren Ambitionen, beste Leistung oder ihr persönliches Lebensmotto, aber sie weisen Aspekte ihres Lebens auf: Deadlines und Rechnungen, Netzwerke und Temperament, Erziehung und Umgebung und ihre künstlerischen Entscheidungen.

Vielleicht birgt das die Möglichkeit, die diesem Job eigene Zurückgezogenheit auszugleichen, doch wenn die Illustration erst einmal vom Tisch und verkauft ist, findet man nur selten einen Illustrator, der sich nicht nach Kontakt sehnt. Täglich finden sich Gruppen von Enthusiasten oder professionellen Verbindungen, deren Teilnehmer Tausende von elektronischen Botschaften über die unterschiedlichsten Aspekte ihres Berufs austauschen und ihre Ansichten in sozialen Netzwerken und Online-Verzeichnissen bloggen. Persönliche Begegnungen, seien sie übers Internet vorbereitet oder komplett in virtuellen Gefilden organisiert, werden nun immer häufiger und zugänglicher. Manchmal scheuen sich Illustratoren ein wenig, die eigenen vier Wände zu verlassen, um Kollegen und Gleichgesinnte, Bewunderer und Idole zu treffen, an den in aller Welt organisierten Zeichen-Marathons oder Comic Conventions teilzunehmen, Vorträge und Debatten zu besuchen, Aktsitzungen zu machen oder einfach gemeinsam ein Bier zu trinken – alles in der Hoffnung, vielleicht eine weitere Illustration an den Start zu bekommen.

Darum sind solche Publikationen wie die, die Sie gerade lesen, so wichtig. Sie hilft, Profi-Illustratoren nicht nur mit anderen Menschen, sondern auch mit ihrer eigenen Gegenwart zu verbinden. Hier wird eine Sammlung und Aufzeichnung des „NOW!" in der Illustration geschaffen, um Debatten anzufachen, bekannte und unbekannte Talente zu feiern und zu entdecken. Damit wachsen wir alle weiter und entwickeln uns, indem wir die Welt durch die Augen der anderen sehen. Und in einer Welt voller Bilder, Informationen, Klang und Wut wird auch ein wenig die Einsamkeit des Illustrators gelindert.

Seul dans la foule : l'illustrateur Now !

par Bruno Porto

Père depuis peu d'un merveilleux petit garçon, j'ai commencé à trouver des points communs entre la naissance d'un enfant et celle d'une illustration, les deux pouvant en théorie se produire en solitaire (comme mon travail) ou dans une pièce bruyante remplie de gens et de machines (comme quand Artur est né). Les grossesses commencent en général avec deux personnes (ne rentrons pas plus dans le sujet), mais même si le partenaire est extrêmement présent et participatif, la mère porte l'enfant seule. De façon semblable, la tâche d'un illustrateur m'a toujours parue solitaire.

Tel est le cas non seulement des artistes qui s'évertuent seuls dans leur studio, mais aussi de ceux qui travaillent en équipe ou en partenariat avec d'autres illustrateurs, directeurs artistiques/créatifs, concepteurs, éditeurs ou écrivains. Le simple fait de poser un outil sur une surface (un crayon sur du papier, un pinceau sur une toile, un stylet sur une tablette) est une action qui se fait en solitaire. Comme la femme enceinte, l'artiste peut se voir entouré mais au final, il est livré à lui-même. La future mère suit les conseils des docteurs, des amis et de Google ; l'artiste est pour sa part orienté par des critères artistiques ou budgétaires, quand il s'inspire d'une photographie, interprète un manuscrit, suit des instructions établies il y a plusieurs décennies ou simplement, pour se divertir, passe d'une ligne à l'autre.

Que la source soit donc externe ou interne, l'illustrateur porte l'illustration en lui-même et devra y faire mentalement face seul. En quête de plusieurs façons de créer une représentation visuelle artificielle (à savoir, de l'ART) d'un aspect de la réalité, son esprit canalise toutes les connaissances, références et expériences tant personnelles que professionnelles qu'il a acquises depuis son premier gribouillage, et les conjugue avec les outils, l'humeur, les délais, les aspirations du moment, etc. Brouillon ou copie finale, l'œuvre connaîtra sans doute des interférences extérieures (encreur, coloriste, éditeur, concepteur, imprimeur, censeur), mais peut aussi atteindre sa destination finale en ayant conservé toute son intégrité.

Malgré cela, comme les bébés, les illustrations sont à l'image de leurs illustrateurs. Sans parler forcément de leurs ambitions, de leur potentiel ou de leur devise, elles reflètent au moins certains aspects de leur vie : leurs délais, leurs factures, leur réseau, leur caractère, leur éducation, leur environnement, leurs choix artistiques.

Pour compenser l'isolement du travail, une fois l'illustration sortie du four, il est rare qu'un illustrateur ne recherche pas le contact. Chaque jour, des membres de groupes de passionnés ou d'associations professionnelles échangent des milliers de messages sur les différents aspects de leur profession et publient leurs opinions sur des réseaux sociaux et des répertoires en ligne. Les rencontres, annoncées en ligne, entièrement virtuelles ou en face à face, sont devenues plus courantes et accessibles. Parfois un peu timide, l'illustrateur quitte sa tanière pour rencontrer ses pairs, ses admirateurs et ses idoles à l'occasion de randocroquis à travers le monde, de salons de la bande dessinée, de conférences et de débats, de séances de dessin d'après modèle, ou tout simplement autour d'une bière. Avec l'espoir de créer une nouvelle illustration.

C'est pourquoi les publications comme celle que vous êtes en train de lire sont si importantes. Elles permettent de mettre en contact les professionnels de l'illustration avec d'autres personnes, mais aussi avec leur époque. Pour créer une archive des illustrations du moment présent, pour alimenter le débat, pour rendre hommage à des talents connus et méconnus, pour nous permettre d'évoluer en voyant le monde à travers le regard d'autrui. Et aussi pour combattre un peu la solitude de l'illustrateur dans un monde rempli d'images, d'informations, de sons et de rage.

Illustration Now Not Then

by Steven Heller

My ignorance is revealed each time I make the prediction that the *Illustration Now!* series has reached the end of a very successful run. I should know by now, for invariably editor Julius Wiedemann calls triumphantly to announce the next installment is finished – and asks if I might rise to the challenge of writing another foreword. I cannot refuse the godfather.

Wiedemann is always finding new ways to expand the taxonomies of illustration. In addition to editing this fourth volume in 7 years, he oversaw another one devoted entirely to portraits which was published earlier this year with just as much weight and heft as the omnibus volumes. This collection of around 150 new illustrators – some veterans but many neophytes – belies the persistent fallacy that illustration is a dying art form. While the outlets for certain kinds of editorial and advertising illustration may be drying up, the inclination among artists to create narrative, symbolic, metaphoric, comic, witty, and satirical pictures for mass consumption continues unabated – and perhaps with more vigor than ever.

If examples in this and the previous volumes of *Illustration Now!* are any indication, the inclination is bolstered by a determination to keep illustration a youthful art. This is not to say there is any age-limit on who can practice illustration – some of the finest "contemporary" illustrators (Seymour Chwast, R.O. Blechman) are 80 years old. Their work is full of youthful vigor cut with experience and emotion – and both mentioned have been in previous *Illustration Now!* volumes. By youthful, I mean that illustration "now" is not encased in amber or a slave to past verities. I defy anyone to find anything in this book that is stodgy, timeworn, or antique. If anything it's like walking into a gallery in a hip cultural center.

Sure, there are more than a few retro styles, but irony prevails. Yes, there is craft that echoes the precision of old masters, but why not! And definitely, there are influences that date back to earlier generations, but that is the essence of all art – and especially illustration. This "illustration now" is art of the zeitgeist. While the messages and concepts range across time and space, the word "NOW" is quite apt. There is nothing in this book to suggest "THEN."

When I first became interested in illustration – in fact, I really wanted to be an illustrator but lacked the skills to do so – the Society of Illustrators in New York was the gatekeeper or governing body, so to speak. From its exclusive competitions, exhibitions, and annuals derived the "standards" that defined the profession. Arguably, those standards were rooted in rules of 19th-century painting techniques and illustration narratives. On one side were studio-realist masters like Thomas Eakins and Robert Henri, who handed down hard-learned traditions that dated back to the Renaissance. On the other side were the painter/illustrators, like Winslow Homer and Howard Pyle, who soaked up the inspirations of these past masters and found new means of illuminating old texts. For the better part of the 20th century, illustrators – even the most famous, like Norman Rockwell – carried the DNA of the past. Rockwell, who Brad Holland has called the "American Vermeer," exemplified an American pictorial narrative that was firmly situated in old ideas of art. While his work entertained a contemporary audience, his underpinnings were not modern – in fact, quite anti-modern.

Illustrators tended to save their "modern" or abstract work for Sundays, not for the daily job. Despite the art world's avant-garde adventures, most commercial clients were suspect for injecting progressive art into the average American's visual diet. Until the mid-1950s, when a new generation of expressionist, impressionist, and surrealist illustrators emerged (some influenced by European artists), illustration was a means to romanticize – or simply bolster the *status quo*. Like Soviet Socialist Realism, American realist/romantic illustration was a subversive propaganda tool for insuring semi-official mediocrity.

The generation of conceptual illustrators, now into their early 70s (Marshall Arisman, Robert Grossman, Paul Davis, James McMullan) and 80s (most notably the late Robert Weaver, who would be in his 80s), helped alter the paradigm of conventional illustration from a *status quo* art to a progressive one. While rampant experimentation was impossible in the marketplace, these artists were content to shift the lines in the sand, pushing forward in a continu-

"This 'illustration now' is art of the zeitgeist.
While the messages and concepts range across time
and space, the word 'NOW' is quite apt.
There is nothing in this book to suggest 'THEN.'"

ous motion and incrementally changing popular attitudes about "what is illustration?"

Thirty years ago, *American Illustration* annual was founded as a progressive alternative to the then entrenched Society of Illustrators. At the time, the founders (including me) were in our twenties and thirties and energized to make a "new illustration". Rather than follow the dictates of the Society of Illustrators concerning the standards of original work, *American Illustration* was mostly concerned with the printed piece – and valued smart concept as much as style and form. It allowed for less-mannered approaches, less-finished work, including *l'art brut*, which was on the rise, collage and neo-expressionism. Raw methods co-existed with highly polished ones. The only restriction: the work had to be about "NOW" not "THEN."

Over the thirty-year span illustration has changed and changed again. A revitalized Society of Illustrators is now indistinguishable from *American Illustration*; and *American Illustration*, while retaining its franchise of showcasing younger artists, is inevitably more establishment than alternative. Styles emerge and submerge. Artists of all kinds have contributed to the overall illustration language(s) – some are incredibly original, while others are palpably derivative. The result is an extremely eclectic medium that welcomes almost all approaches (and even embraces Rockwellian approaches if not simply being a digital copy of the old).

Illustration Now! started its own tradition. The first edition was a distinct blend of the progressive old and new. Each subsequent edition shows that talent does not need to be called old or new, for regardless of chronological age, the illustrations therein and herein fit only one specific category and that is "NOW" not "THEN."

Illustration heute, nicht damals

von Steven Heller

Ich stolpere jedes Mal wieder über meine Ignoranz, wenn ich die Vorhersage treffe, die sehr erfolgreiche Reihe *Illustration Now!* sei nun mittlerweile am Ende angekommen. Das sollte ich mittlerweile kapiert haben, denn irgendwann ruft todsicher deren Herausgeber Julius Wiedemann an und verkündet, die nächste Folge der Serie sei fertiggestellt. Und unweigerlich fragt er mich, ob ich mich der Herausforderung stellen wolle, ein weiteres Vorwort zu schreiben. Damit macht er mir ein Angebot, das ich nicht abschlagen kann.

Julius Wiedemann findet stets neue Wege, um die Systematik der Illustration zu erweitern. Neben diesen vier Bänden in sieben Jahren hat er einen weiteren Band betreut, der sich ausschließlich den Porträts widmet. In Umfang und Gewicht steht er den anderen Sammelbänden in nichts nach. Die hier vorliegende Sammlung mit etwa 150 neuen Illustratoren – einige Veteranen, aber viele Neueinsteiger – straft die beharrliche Fehleinschätzung Lügen, dass es sich bei der Illustration um eine sterbende Kunstform handelt. Zwar werden für bestimmte Arten von redaktioneller und Werbeillustration die Absatzgebiete dünner, aber Künstler finden unvermindert erzählerische, symbolische, metaphorische, komische, geistreiche und satirische Bilder für den Massenkonsum – und diese Bilder sind vielleicht sogar noch kraftvoller als je zuvor.

Wenn die Beispiele aus diesem und den vorigen Bänden der Reihe *Illustration Now!* ein Indiz dafür sind, dann wird dieses Streben der Künstler noch durch ihre Entschlossenheit unterstützt, die Illustration als jugendliche Kunst zu bewahren. Das bedeutet nun nicht, dass es eine Altersgrenze gibt, bis zu der man Illustrationen machen darf – einige der besten „zeitgenössischen" Illustratoren wie Seymour Chwast oder R. O. Blechman sind 80 Jahre alt. Ihre Arbeiten sind voller jugendlicher Vitalität, getränkt mit Erfahrung und Emotion – und die beiden eben Genannten wurden auch in den anderen Bänden von *Illustration Now!* vorgestellt. Mit „jugendlich" meine ich, dass Illustration „jetzt" nicht in Stein gemeißelt ist oder sklavisch an vergangenen Wahrheiten hängt. Ich werde jeden zur Rede stellen, der meint, in diesem Buch irgendetwas schwer Verdauliches, Abgenutztes oder Antiquiertes zu finden. Wenn überhaupt,

ist dieser Band wie ein Spaziergang in der Galerie eines hippen Kulturzentrums.

Sicher, hier finden sich durchaus einige Retro-Stile, aber die Ironie bleibt weiterhin vorherrschend. Ja, sicher gibt es Beispiele, in denen das Handwerk die Präzision alter Meister widerspiegelt, aber warum auch nicht? Und es gibt definitiv einen Einfluss früherer Generationen, doch so ist das Wesen aller Kunst – und insbesondere das der Illustration. Dieser Band aus der Reihe *Illustration Now!* zeigt die Kunst des Zeitgeistes. Botschaften und Konzepte mögen sich in Raum und Zeit verändern, aber das Wort „NOW" ist nach wie vor ziemlich passend. In diesem Buch findet sich nichts, was an ein „THEN" denken ließe.

Als ich mich zum ersten Mal für die Illustration interessierte (tatsächlich wollte ich mal Illustrator werden, doch mir fehlten dafür Geschick und Talent), war die *Society of Illustrators* in New York sozusagen Türhüter oder Dachverband. Aus ihren exklusiven Wettbewerben, Ausstellungen und Jahrbüchern leiteten sich die „Standards" ab, die den Berufsstand definierten. Zweifellos wurzelten diese Standards in Regeln über Maltechniken und die Erzählweise von Illustrationen aus dem 19. Jahrhundert. Auf der einen Seite waren es die Meister der realistischen Kunst wie Thomas Eakins und Robert Henri, die hart erlernte, bis in die Renaissance zurückreichende Traditionen weitergaben. Auf der anderen Seite standen Maler und Illustratoren wie Winslow Homer und Howard Pyle, die die Inspirationen dieser alten Meister aufsogen und neue Wege fanden, um alte Texte zu illustrieren. Im 20. Jahrhundert trugen die Illustratoren – sogar die bedeutendsten wie Norman Rockwell – meist die DNA der Vergangenheit in sich. Rockwell, der von Brad Holland als „amerikanischer Vermeer" bezeichnet wurde, stand für eine amerikanische bildliche Erzählung, die fest mit den alten Ideen von Kunst verbunden war. Während sich ein zeitgenössisches Publikum von seinen Arbeiten unterhalten ließ, waren seine Wurzeln gar nicht so modern – tatsächlich sogar ziemlich antimodern.

Die Illustratoren neigten dazu, ihre „modernen" oder abstrakten Arbeiten für den Sonntag aufzusparen und nicht in die alltäglichen Arbeiten einfließen zu lassen. Trotz der

„Dieser Band aus der Reihe Illustration Now! *zeigt die Kunst des Zeitgeistes.*
Botschaften und Konzepte mögen sich in Raum und Zeit verändern,
aber das Wort ‚NOW' ist nach wie vor ziemlich passend.
In diesem Buch findet sich nichts, was an ein ‚THEN' denken ließe."

Avantgardeabenteuer der Kunstwelt waren die meisten
kommerziellen Kunden misstrauisch, wenn es darum ging,
eine progressive Kunst in die visuellen Konsumgewohnhei-
ten des Durchschnittsamerikaners einzuführen. Bis Mitte
der 50er-Jahre, als eine neue Generation von expressionisti-
schen, impressionistischen und surrealistischen Illustratoren
in Erscheinung trat (manche beeinflusst von europäischen
Künstlern), war die Illustration ein Mittel zur Verklä-
rung – oder einfach eine Möglichkeit, um den *Status quo*
zu unterstützen. Wie beim sozialistischen Realismus der
Sowjets war die amerikanische realistische bzw. romantische
Illustration ein subversives Propagandainstrument, um eine
halb offizielle Mittelmäßigkeit zu gewährleisten.

Die Generation der konzeptionellen Illustratoren, die
wie Marshall Arisman, Robert Grossman, Paul Davis und
James McMullan nun mittlerweile in ihren Siebzigern und
Achtzigern ist (hier ist besonders der verstorbene Robert
Weaver zu nennen, der heute beinahe neunzig Jahre alt
wäre), half dabei, das Paradigma der konventionellen Illustration von einer Kunst des *Status quo* hin zu einer progres-
siven Kunst zu verändern. Zwar konnte man auf dem Markt
und im Kundenkontakt unmöglich zügellos experimentieren, aber die Künstler begnügten sich damit, in einer
gleitenden Bewegung und schrittweisen Veränderung sanft
die Grenzen zu verwischen und damit auch die allgemeinen
Ansichten darüber, was Illustrationen sind.

Vor dreißig Jahren wurde das Jahrbuch *American Illustration* als progressive Alternative zur *Society of Illustrators*
gegründet, die damals fest etabliert war. Zu jener Zeit waren
die Gründer, zu denen auch ich zählte, in ihren Zwanzigern
und Dreißigern und drängten darauf, „neue Illustrationen"
zu schaffen. Anstatt dem Diktat der *Society of Illustrators*
zu folgen, das sich mit den Standards von Originalen
beschäftigte, beschäftigte sich *American Illustration* vor allem
mit dem gedruckten Werk – und man schätzte ein cleveres
Konzept genauso hoch ein wie Stil und Form. Erlaubt waren aber auch weniger gekünstelte Herangehensweisen oder
unfertigere Arbeiten, darunter auch die *Art brut*, die gerade
im Kommen war, Collagen und neoexpressionistische Wer-
ke. Bodenständige Techniken standen gleichrangig neben

höchst ausgefeilten Arbeiten. Die einzige Einschränkung:
Die Arbeit musste sich mit „NOW" beschäftigen und nicht
mit „THEN".

Im Laufe von dreißig Jahren hat sich die Illustration
immer wieder gewandelt und verändert. Die neu belebte
Society of Illustrators kann man nun von *American Illustration*
nicht mehr unterscheiden; Letzteres bewahrt zwar sein An-
recht, jüngere Künstler zu präsentieren, ist aber unweigerlich eher etabliert als alternativ. Stile tauchen auf und gehen
wieder unter. Künstler aller Art tragen zu einer übergreifen-
den illustrativen Sprache bei – manch eine ist unglaublich
originell, andere Sprachen hingegen lassen sich eindeutig
ableiten. Das Ergebnis ist ein extrem eklektisches Medium,
in dem beinahe alle Ansätze willkommen sind (und in
dem sogar ein Rockwell'sches Vorgehen seinen Platz findet,
wenn es nicht bloß eine digitale Kopie des Alten darstellt).

Illustration Now! hat seine eigene Tradition geschaffen.
Die erste Ausgabe war eine ausgeprägte Mischung des
progressiv Alten und Neuen. Jede folgende Ausgabe zeigt,
dass man ein Talent nicht als neu oder alt bezeichnen muss,
denn ungeachtet des zeitlichen Alters passen die Illustrationen hier wie dort nur in eine spezielle Kategorie, und die
lautet „NOW" und nicht „THEN".

L'illustration d'aujourd'hui et non d'hier

par Steven Heller

Mon ignorance est mise en évidence chaque fois que je prédis la fin de la brillante série *Illustration Now!*. Je devrais pourtant le savoir à ce stade, car l'éditeur Julius Wiedemann ne manque jamais d'appeler, triomphant, pour annoncer que le prochain volume est terminé et demander si je veux relever le défi d'écrire l'avant-propos. L'offre est impossible à refuser.

Wiedemann trouve toujours des moyens inédits de développer les taxonomies de l'illustration. Outre l'édition de ce quatrième volume en 7 ans, il en a supervisé un autre entièrement consacré aux portraits, publié plus tôt cette année avec autant de poids que les volumes généralistes. Cette collection d'environ 150 nouveaux illustrateurs, avec quelques vétérans et beaucoup de néophytes, dément l'éternel sophisme selon lequel l'illustration serait une forme d'art mourante. Même si les débouchés de certains types d'illustration pour l'édition ou la publicité s'essoufflent, la tendance des artistes à créer des images narratives, symboliques, métaphoriques, drôles, spirituelles et satiriques pour la consommation de masse se poursuit sans relâche, voire avec encore plus de vigueur.

Les exemples de ce volume d'*Illustration Now!* et des antérieurs montrent bien que ce penchant est nourri par la volonté de renouveler sans cesse l'art de l'illustration. Cela ne veut absolument pas dire qu'il y aurait une limite d'âge pour la pratique de l'illustration : certains des plus grands illustrateurs « contemporains » (Seymour Chwast, R.O. Blechman) sont octogénaires. Leur travail affiche une énergie juvénile assortie d'expérience et d'émotion, deux aspects déjà présents dans les précédents volumes d'*Illustration Now!*. Par juvénile, j'entends que l'illustration « actuelle » n'est pas figée dans l'ambre, ni esclave de vérités passées. Je défie quiconque de trouver dans cet ouvrage quoi que ce soit de pesant, rebattu ou démodé. Tout évoque la visite d'une galerie dans un centre culturel en vogue.

Il y a évidemment des styles rétro, mais l'ironie l'emporte. Certaines œuvres rappellent sans conteste la précision des grands maîtres, mais pourquoi pas ! Et bien sûr, certaines influences remontent à des générations passées, mais c'est là toute l'essence de l'art, et en particulier de l'illustration.

Cette illustration actuelle est l'art de l'air du temps. Bien que les messages et les concepts s'étalent dans le temps et l'espace, le concept de « NOW » est assez approprié. Rien dans cet ouvrage ne suggère le passé.

Quand j'ai commencé à m'intéresser à l'illustration (en fait, je voulais devenir illustrateur mais manquais de talent pour le faire), la Society of Illustrators de New York était l'entité directrice, pour ainsi dire. Des compétitions, expositions et publications exclusives qu'elle organisait naissaient les « normes » régissant la profession, des normes ancrées dans des techniques de peinture et des théories illustratives du XIXe siècle. Il y avait, d'un côté, les maîtres du réalisme comme Thomas Eakins et Robert Henri, qui transmettaient les traditions apprises depuis la Renaissance ; de l'autre, les peintres/illustrateurs comme Winslow Homer et Howard Pyle, qui s'inspiraient de ces maîtres et inventaient de nouvelles façons d'enluminer des textes anciens. Pendant une grande partie du XXe siècle, les illustrateurs, y compris les plus célèbres comme Norman Rockwell, portaient l'ADN du passé. Rockwell, que Brad Holland a surnommé le « Vermeer américain », représentait une histoire picturale américaine profondément attachée à la vieille école de l'art. Ses œuvres ont conquis un public contemporain, mais leur fondation n'était pas moderne, justement plutôt antimoderne.

Les illustrateurs avaient tendance à garder leurs créations « modernes » ou abstraites pour le dimanche, mais pas pour la production quotidienne. Malgré les aventures avant-gardistes du monde artistique, la plupart des clients commerciaux étaient soupçonnés d'injecter de l'art progressif dans le régime visuel de l'Américain moyen. Jusqu'au milieu des années 1950, quand une nouvelle génération d'illustrateurs expressionnistes, impressionnistes et surréalistes a vu le jour (certains influencés par des artistes européens), l'illustration servait à romancer, ou simplement à entretenir le *statu quo*. Comme le réalisme socialiste soviétique, l'illustration réaliste/romantique américaine était un outil de propagande subversif pour garantir une médiocrité semi-officielle.

La génération des illustrateurs conceptuels, aujourd'hui septuagénaires (Marshall Arisman, Robert Grossman, Paul Davis, James McMullan) et octogénaires (en particulier

*« Cette illustration actuelle est l'art de l'air du temps.
Bien que les messages et les concepts s'étalent dans le temps
et l'espace, le concept de ‹ NOW › est assez approprié.
Rien dans cet ouvrage ne suggère le passé. »*

Robert Weaver, qui aurait aujourd'hui plus de 80 ans),
a contribué à changer le paradigme de l'illustration
conventionnelle, passant d'un art figé à un art progressif.
Comme le marché ne permettait pas une expérimentation
exubérante, ces artistes ont dû progresser avec plus de subti-
lité, en repoussant graduellement les limites et en modifiant
patiemment les attitudes du public sur ce qu'impliquait
l'illustration.

Il y a trente ans, la publication annuelle *American Illustration* a été lancée comme réponse progressiste à l'indélo-
geable Society of Illustrators. À cette époque, ses fondateurs
(dont je faisais partie) avaient la vingtaine et la trentaine, et
étaient bien décidés à créer une « nouvelle illustration ». Au
lieu d'obéir aux dictats de la Society of Illustrators en ma-
tière des standards de l'œuvre originale, *American Illustration*
s'attachait surtout à l'œuvre imprimée et accordait autant de
valeur à un concept intelligent qu'au style et à la forme. Ceci
autorisait des approches moins mièvres, des créations moins
achevées (dont l'art brut, en pleine ascension), des collages
et du néo-expressionnisme. Des méthodes brutes cohabi-
taient avec d'autres très sophistiquées. La seule restriction
était que le travail devait être actuel, et abandonner le passé.

Au fil de ces trente années, l'illustration n'a cessé de
changer et d'évoluer. Revitalisée, la Society of Illustrators
est désormais le calque d'*American Illustration*, laquelle,
bien que continuant à faire connaître de jeunes artistes, est
inévitablement devenue plus conformiste. Des styles naissent
et meurent. Des artistes en tous genres ont contribué au(x)
langage(s) de l'illustration : certains sont extrêmement originaux, d'autres manifestement moins. Le résultat est un art
extrêmement éclectique qui englobe quasiment toutes les approches (y compris celles d'influence Rockwellienne, s'il ne
s'agit pas uniquement d'une copie numérique de l'original).

Illustration Now! a lancé une nouvelle tradition. Le premier volume offrait un mélange d'art progressif nouveau et
ancien. Ceux qui ont suivi ont montré que le talent n'a pas
besoin d'être qualifié de nouveau ou d'ancien. Car quelle
que soit leur position dans la chronologie, les illustrations
de tous les volumes de cette série appartiennent à une seule
catégorie : l'art d'aujourd'hui, et non d'hier.

↓   Metal Man, by Paul Hoppe, 2008,
Charlesbridge Publishing, Art Direction:
Susan Sherman; mixed media

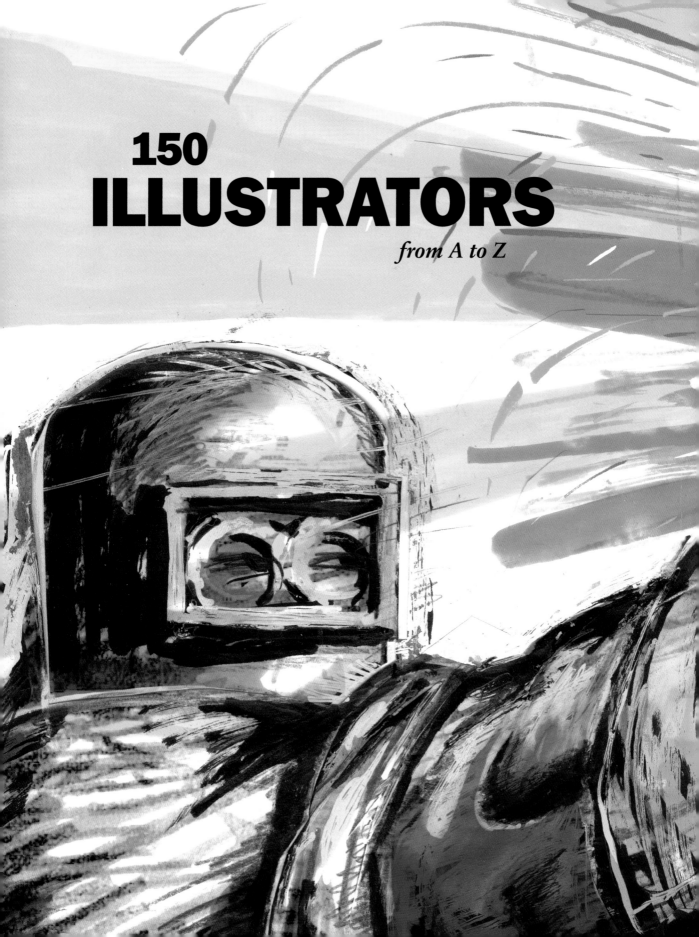
150
ILLUSTRATORS
from A to Z

Eda Akaltun

1985 born in Istanbul, Turkey | lives and works in London, United Kingdom

AGENT
Heart
London, New York
www.heartagency.com

"Old photos and magazines inspire me because of their colours, textures and fashions. I use these to create futuristic, false-perspective environments."

„Alte Fotos und Magazine inspirieren mich wegen ihrer Farben, Texturen und Moden. Daraus schaffe ich futuristische Umgebungen mit falschen Perspektiven."

« Les couleurs, les textures et la mode des vieilles photos et des magazines poussiéreux m'inspirent. Je m'en sers pour créer des environnements futuristes avec de fausses perspectives. »

↑   Squared Harmony, 2010,
personal work; digital collage

→   Quantum Loopholes, 2011,
New Scientist magazine; digital collage

→→ Incurable Soul, 2010, personal
work; digital collage and marbling

↑   Blue Ocean Fiction, 2011,
Harvard Business Review magazine;
digital collage

←   Buying Time, 2011,
Eye magazine; digital collage

→→ The Part-Time Job, 2010,
New Statesman magazine; digital collage

Daniel Almeida

1975 born in Ribeirão Preto (SP), Brazil | lives and works in São Paulo (SP), Brazil
www.danielalmeida.art.br

*"Funny, ironic, handmade look,
contemporary-vintage mood."*

„*Lustiger, ironischer, handgemachter Look,
zeitgenössisch-altmodische Stimmung.*"

« *Un look artisanal, drôle et ironique,
une touche contemporaine et vintage.* »

↑   Monster #1, 2010, personal work;
hand-drawing and Adobe Photoshop

→   Is Coca-Cola addictive?, 2010,
Galileu magazine; hand-drawing
and Adobe Photoshop

→→ Monster #3, 2010, personal work;
hand-drawing and Adobe Photoshop

Martin Ansin

1977 born in Montevideo, Uruguay | lives and works in Montevideo, Uruguay
www.martinansin.com

AGENT
Gerald & Cullen Rapp
New York
www.rappart.com

↑   Scott Pilgrim vs. the World, 2010,
The Alamo Drafthouse, poster;
hand-drawing and digital

→   The Flaming Lips – Dark Side
of the Moon, 2010, *Playboy* magazine;
hand-drawing and digital

→→ The Social Network, 2010, *Wired*
magazine; hand-drawing and digital

*"Drawing a bull's nose is as
complicated as drawing a human
ear. Actually, I just did the nose
in the manner of an ear
and it worked."*

„Eine Stierschnauze ist so kompliziert zu
zeichnen wie ein menschliches Ohr. Tatsächlich
habe ich die Nase so wie ein Ohr gemacht,
und es hat funktioniert."

« Il est aussi compliqué de dessiner le museau
d'un taureau qu'une oreille humaine.
En fait, j'ai dessiné le museau comme une
oreille et ça a marché. »

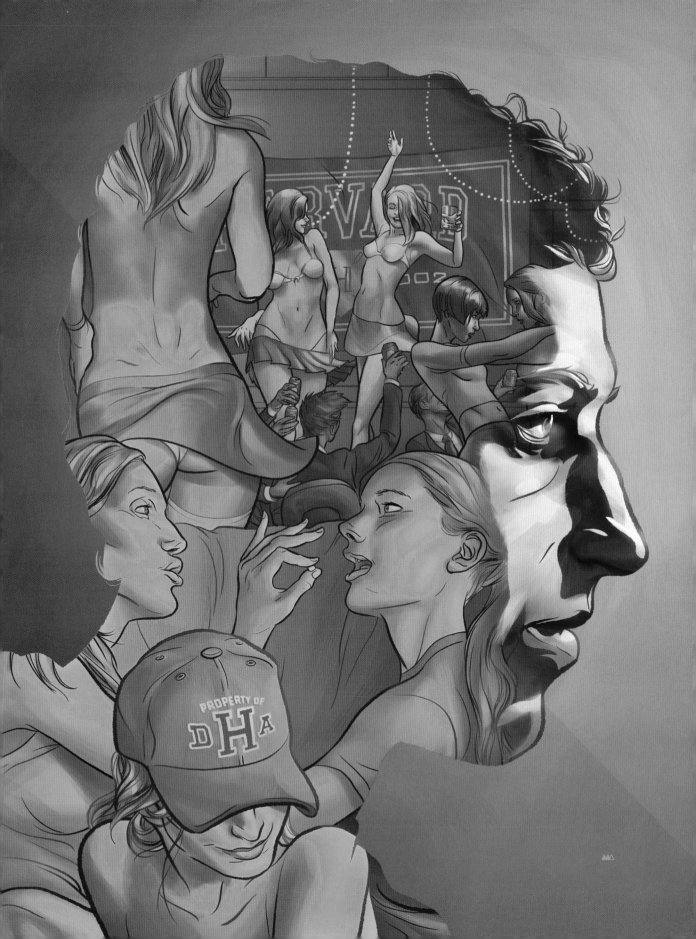

Frank Arbelo

1965 born in Manzanillo, Cuba | lives and works in La Paz, Bolivia
http://frankarbelo.blogspot.com

EXHIBITIONS

1. "El Emigrante",
Espacio Simón I. Patiño,
La Paz, 2010

2. "La Fiesta Pagana",
Espacio Simón I. Patiño,
La Paz, 2008

3. Internacional Poster
Biennal of Mexico, 2006

4. Festival Internacional
de Historietas, La Paz, 2004

5. "Trabajos", solo show,
C+C Espacio, La Paz, 2003

"I try to make sure my illustrations are clear and that they complete the story they illustrate."

„*Ich achte möglichst darauf, dass meine Illustrationen klar und deutlich sind und dass sie die Story abrunden, die sie illustrieren sollen.*"

« *Je m'efforce de créer des illustrations claires et complétant l'histoire qu'elles accompagnent.* »

↑   The Fighter, 2006, personal work,
self-promotion postcards; pencil, ink
and digital colour

→   Beautiful, 2008, personal work;
pencil, ink and digital colour

→→ Punk!, 2007, *La Ronckanblus*
magazine; pencil, ink and digital colour

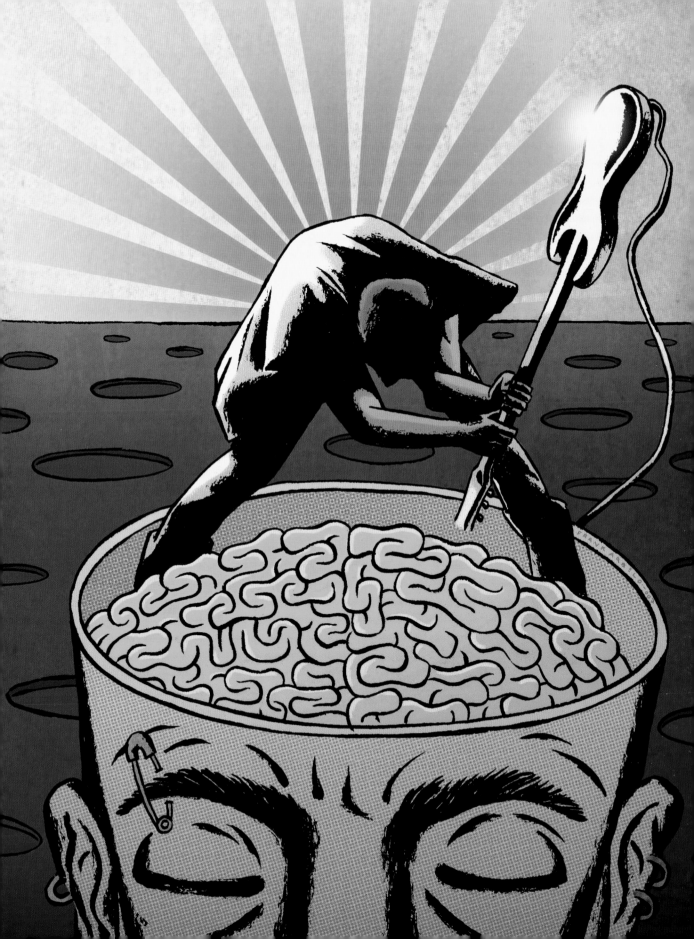

André Azevedo

1978 born in Curitiba (PR), Brazil | lives and works in Curitiba (PR), Brazil
http://andreazevedoart.blogspot.com

EXHIBITIONS

1. "Héritage", group show, Lacoste's Project, Rio de Janeiro, 2010

2. The Affordable Art Fair, New York, 2009

3. Brazilian Design Biennial, Curitiba, 2007

"I love the combination of drawing, painting and sewing on to fabrics, and also playing with sculpture, photography and cinema."

„Ich liebe es, Zeichnen, Malen und Nähen auf Stoffen zu kombinieren, und spiele gerne mit Skulpturen, Fotografie und Kino."

«J'adore mélanger le dessin, la peinture et la couture sur des tissus, et aussi toucher à la sculpture, à la photographie et au cinéma. »

↑   Untitled, 2010, OnSpeed, website; drawing and sewing

→→   Untitled, 2009, personal work; drawing and sewing

Chico Baldini

1976 born in Porto Alegre (RS), Brazil | lives and works in Porto Alegre (RS) and in São Paulo (SP), Brazil
www.chicobaldini.com.br

EXHIBITIONS

1. Cow Parade, São Paulo, 2010
2. Diarios Visuais, solo show, Porto Alegre, 2009
3. Casa Cor, São Paulo, 2009
4. Grafica Trindade, Porto Alegre, 2008

"I've been addicted to drawing as long as I can remember and always try to keep a sketchbook with me for drawing in my spare time, whenever I have the opportunity."

„Solange ich denken kann, bin ich regelrecht süchtig nach Zeichnen. Ich habe möglichst immer ein Skizzenbuch bei mir, damit ich auch in meiner Freizeit zeichnen kann, wenn sich die Gelegenheit ergibt."

« J'ai toujours aimé dessiner et j'ai constamment sur moi un bloc pour dessiner pendant mon temps libre, chaque fois que l'occasion se présente. »

↑ Untitled, 2009, personal work; hand-drawing and Adobe Photoshop

→→ Untitled, 2009, personal work; hand-drawing and Adobe Photoshop

Olivier Balez

1972 born in Besançon, France | lives and works in Santiago, Chile and in Nice, France
www.olivierbalez.com

AGENT 1
Prima Linea
Paris
www.primalinea.com

AGENT 2
French Touch Agency
San Francisco
www.frenchtouchagency.net

EXHIBITIONS
1. "Living with Earthquakes", National Library, Santiago, 2011

2. "Children's Books Illustrations", San Francisco Public Library, 2005

3. "Jazz Drawings", Sunset Jazz Club, Paris, 1997

"Simplicity is a difficult equilibrium between nothing left to add and nothing left to take away."

„*Einfachheit ist die schwierige Balance zwischen dem, was man nicht mehr hinzufügen, und dem, was man nicht mehr wegnehmen kann.*"

« *La simplicité est un équilibre délicat entre ne rien avoir à ajouter et ne rien avoir à enlever.* »

↑　Sheherazade, 2010, Editions Sarbacane, children's book; Adobe Photoshop

→→　La cordée du Mont Rose, 2010, *XXI* magazine, Art Direction: Quintin Leeds and Sara Deux; Adobe Photoshop

Jonathan Ball

1974 born in Cardiff, United Kingdom | lives and works in Cardiff, United Kingdom
www.pokedstudio.com

AGENT 1
Jelly London
London
www.jellylondon.com

AGENT 2
Mendola Art
New York
www.mendolaart.com

AGENT 3
Ammo
Stockholm
www.ammo.se

EXHIBITIONS
1. "Sho-me Illustration", Cardiff, 2011
2. "Rasterizing", Recoat Gallery, Glasgow, 2009
3. "Make feat. Beautiful", Lafayette, Paris, 2008

"In a small corner of Pixel Town, vector meets cute, meets madness and meets danger. Mix it all up and shake it up and down, and pour it all out."

„In einem kleinen Winkel von Pixel Town trifft Vektor auf Süß, auf Wahnsinn und auf Gefahr. Alles gut mischen, kräftig schütteln und dann ausgießen."

« Dans un coin de Pixel Town, le vecteur rencontre la beauté, la folie et le danger. Mélangez le tout et secouez bien avant de servir. »

↑ Welcome to Hell, 2010, personal work; Adobe Illustrator and Adobe Photoshop

→→ Monster of Rock, 2010, personal work; 3D render and Adobe Photoshop

Adhemas Batista

1980 born in São Paulo (SP), Brazil | lives and works in Los Angeles (CA), USA
www.adhemas.com

*"Bold and glorious with all the colorful flourish
and passion of any Brazilian carnival scene."*

*„Schwungvoll und prächtig mit all den Schnörkeln und der
Leidenschaft einer Karnevalsszene irgendwo in Brasilien."*

*« Audacieux et somptueux avec les explosions de couleur
et la passion d'une scène de carnaval brésilien. »*

↑ Feet, 2010, personal work; digital

→→ Twins, 2010, *Serafina* magazine; digital

Larissa Bertonasco

1972 born in Heilbronn, Germany | lives and works in Hamburg, Germany
www.bertonasco.de

AGENT
Susanne Koppe
Hamburg
www.auserlesen-
ausgezeichnet.de

EXHIBITIONS
1. "Fumetto", solo show, International Comic Festival, Luzern

2. "La nonna", solo show, Lettres du monde, Literature Festival, Bordeaux

3. "Aus dem Osten in den Süden", solo show, Feinkunst Krüger, Hamburg

4. "La nonna", solo show, Kinderbuchhaus, Altonaer Museum, Hamburg

5. "Spring", group show, Neurotitan, Berlin

"I love typography and use it as an element of design and content, mostly handmade or as a collage. It is very important for me to do manual work because it's the only way I can really connect to the creative process."

„Ich liebe Typografie und setze sie gerne als gestalterisches und inhaltliches Element ein, meist handgemacht oder als Collage. Handwerklich zu arbeiten ist mir sehr wichtig, nur so kann ich mich wirklich mit dem kreativen Prozess verbinden."

« J'aime la typographie et je l'utilise comme un élément graphique et de contenu, le plus souvent à la main ou sous forme de collage. Le travail manuel est très important pour moi car c'est la seule façon que j'ai de connecter avec le processus de création. »

↑ Vache, 2008, *Le Fooding*, restaurant guide; acrylic and stamp

→→ Ferrari, 2010, Jacoby & Stuart, book; acrylic and collage

Luke Best

1977 born in London, United Kingdom | lives and works in London, United Kingdom
www.lukebest.com

AGENT
Heart
London
www.heartagency.com

EXHIBITIONS
1. "It's a Long Way Back",
Krets Gallery, Malmö

2. "Pick Me Up",
Somerset House, London

3. "150 years of the V&A",
Victoria & Albert Museum,
London

4. "93ft of Peepshow",
Jaguar Shoes, London

5. "In between",
Dream Space, London

*"I aim to create images that
have a feeling of unease,
a dysfunctional narrative
and the invisible made visible."*

*„Ich mache es mir zum Ziel, Bilder zu schaffen,
denen ein Gefühl des Unbehagens eigen ist,
die als Erzählung dysfunktional sind
und das Unsichtbare sichtbar machen."*

*« Je tente de créer des images qui expriment
un sentiment de malaise, une problématique,
l'invisible rendu visible. »*

↑   The Sexes, 2011, *The Independent*
newspaper; mixed media

→   Failure, 2011, *HBR* magazine;
mixed media

→→ Porn, 2010, *Therapy* magazine;
mixed media

↑   Curse of the Whale, 2010, *Nobrow*;
mixed media

→→ Taxidermy, 2010, *The Washington Post*
newspaper; mixed media

↑   Harper's, 2010, *Harper's* magazine;
mixed media

Jörg Block

1974 born in Siegburg, Germany | lives and works in Hamburg, Germany
www.joergblock.de

"Illustration plays with associations. I find the contrast between the prosaic allure of vector graphics and hidden meanings very exciting."

„Illustration spielt mit Assoziationen. Dabei reizt mich der Kontrast zwischen dem nüchternen Charme einer Vektorgrafik und den hintergründigen Bedeutungen."

« L'illustration joue avec les associations. Je trouve extrêmement intéressant le contraste entre l'aspect prosaïque des images vectorielles et les significations cachées. »

↑   Baumauto, 2007, personal work, calendar; Adobe Illustrator

→   Ugg Boots, 2011, *Hamburger Abendblatt* magazine; Adobe Illustrator

→→ Meer 1, 2010, personal work, poster; Adobe Illustrator

Nigel Buchanan

1958 born in Gore, New Zealand | lives and works in Sydney, Australia
www.nigelbuchanan.com

AGENT 1
Folio Art
London
www.folioart.co.uk

AGENT 2
Gerald & Cullen Rapp
New York
www.rappart.com

AGENT 3
The Jacky Winter Group
Melbourne
www.jackywinter.com

"Satire and humour makes the ideal choice for me."

„Satire und Humor sind für mich die ideale Wahl."

« La satire et l'humour sont un choix idéal pour moi. »

↑   Flags, 2010, *Reader's Digest* magazine;
pencil and digital

→   Lion Zebra, 2010, *Plansponsor*
magazine; pencil and digital

→→ Bikini, 2004, *BRW* magazine;
pencil and digital

→→ Philanthropist, 2010, *Good Weekend* magazine; pencil and digital

← Angry, 2010, *Plansponsor* magazine; pencil and digital

↙ QSS, 2011, Queen Street Studio, advertising; pencil and digital

↓ Korea, 2008, Grey Advertising, advertising; pencil and digital

Budor & Cule

2006 founded | live and work in New York (NY), USA
www.doraandmaja.com

EXHIBITIONS

1. Anti Design Festival, Redchurch Street, London, 2010

2. Young Guns 7 Awards, Art Directors Club Gallery, New York, 2009

3. Biennale des Jeunes Créateurs d'Europe et de la Méditeranée, Puglia, 2008

4. Zgraf 10, International Festival of Creative Communications, Zagreb, 2008

5. Magdalena, International Festival of Creative Communications, Maribor, 2008

"Our inspiration comes from everyday situations, quotidian phenomena, but also invented narratives and constructed realities with a humorous touch."

„Unsere Inspiration wurzelt in Situationen des Alltags, alltäglichen Phänomenen, aber auch in erfundenen Geschichten und konstruierten Realitäten mit humorvoller Note."

« Nous puisons notre inspiration dans les situations et les phénomènes quotidiens, mais aussi dans les histoires et les réalités inventées avec une touche d'humour. »

↑ The Cult of French (Fries&Manicure) Durational Performance in Hamam, 2011, Sirup Club, New Year's party invitation; handmade paper collage, digital collage

→→ You Are a Beautiful Architectural Ruin, 2010, *Scalpel* magazine; Adobe Photoshop

↑　Winter Scenery, 2010, Sirup Club,
New Year's party invitation; collage

↑ Not That Bad Romance, 2010,
Scalpel magazine; Adobe Photoshop

→ Trippple Nippples: PPP, 2010,
Trippple Nippples, album cover;
acrylic painting, digital collage

George Butler

1985 born in London, United Kingdom | lives and works in London, United Kingdom
www.georgebutler.org

EXHIBITIONS

1. Royal Institute of
Painters in Watercolours,
Mall Galleries, London,
2011, 2009, 2008

2. "Drawn to Africa",
solo show, The Air
Gallery, London, 2010

3. Compton Cassey Gallery,
with Jonathan Poole
and Auguste Rodin and
A.R. Penck

*"My work is based entirely on travelling, reportage
and the location drawing. The more obscure
the subject the better it is."*

*„Meine Arbeit basiert komplett auf Reisen, Reportagen
und dem Zeichnen vor Ort. Je obskurer
das Thema, desto besser."*

*« Mon travail repose essentiellement sur les voyages,
les reportages et les croquis. Plus le sujet
est obscur, mieux c'est. »*

↑ Little boy, Lagos, Nigeria, 2010,
The Times online, "Drawn to Africa"
exhibition catalogue; pen and ink

→→ Lagos Market, Nigeria, 2010,
The Times online, "Drawn to Africa"
exhibition catalogue; pen and ink

John Jay Cabuay

1974 born in Manila, Philippines | lives and works in New York (NY), USA
www.johnjayart.com

AGENT 1
Shannon Associates
New York
www.shannonassociates.com

AGENT 2
Agent 002
Paris
www.agent002.com

EXHIBITIONS
1. "Visual Poetry",
group show, Gallery
Hanahou, New York, 2011

2. Icon 6, Gallery Nucleus,
Alhambra (CA), 2010

3. Society of Illustrators,
Los Angeles, Annual Show,
2009–2011

"My illustrations are about celebrating the art of draftsmanship mixed with the complexity of a saturated color palette and the idealism of print-making."

„In meinen Illustrationen geht es darum, die Kunst des Zeichnens mit der Komplexität einer satten Farbpalette und dem Idealismus der Druckherstellung zu mischen."

« Mes illustrations sont un hommage à l'art du dessin, ajouté à la complexité d'une palette de couleurs saturées et à l'idéalisme de la gravure. »

↑   Mr. T, 2011, personal work;
mixed media and Adobe Photoshop

→   Mandela, 2009, personal work;
mixed media and Adobe Photoshop

→→ The 14th Dalai Lama, 2009, personal
work; mixed media and Adobe Photoshop

↓↓ Saturday Night, 2009, personal work;
mixed media and Adobe Photoshop

Chris Capuozzo

1966 born in Staten Island (NY), USA | lives and works in Chestnut Ridge (NY), USA
www.intergalactico.com

EXHIBITIONS

1. "The Launching of the Dream Weapon", solo show, Sandra Gering Gallery, New York, 2004

2. "Tedious Limbs", Flynn Farm, Los Angeles, 2004

3. Reas Presents, 3more Gallery, Brooklyn, 2004

4. "Art Show", solo show, Funny Garbage Gallery, New York, 2001

5. National Design Triennial, Cooper-Hewitt Museum, New York, 2000

"I'm comfortable and thrilled to use varying techniques in making pictures. Most crucial is the expressive ability of any given technique I use."

„*Wenn ich Bilder mache, arbeite ich sehr gerne mit verschiedenen Techniken, das ist sehr spannend für mich. Absolut wesentlich sind die expressiven Möglichkeiten der von mir eingesetzten Technik.*"

« *J'adore le fait d'employer plusieurs techniques pour créer des images. L'essentiel est la capacité expressive de chaque technique.* »

↑   Untitled, 2010, personal work; gouache and pencil

→→ Intergalactico Gift Wrap, 2009, personal; mixed media collage

FULL SPECTRUM DOMINANCE

STEREO

CONTRACT # QM-13083

9634 流星人間ゾーン/荒野の少年
THE FOOLISH TERRESTRIAL PERSON SHOULD BECOME EXTINCT
目ソノラマ·APM-5018 ソノシート·ソ
INSTEAD IT MEANS I CONTROL THIS STAR
ゴールデンパピイシリーズ 美 ¥1,500

←← Prg Trigger, 2010, Intergalactico promotional piece; mixed media collage

→ "Fabrication Defect" Tom Zé, Luaka Bop, album cover; ink on paper

↓ Branded to Kill & Tokyo Drifter, Criterion, DVD packaging; pencil on paper and Adobe Illustrator

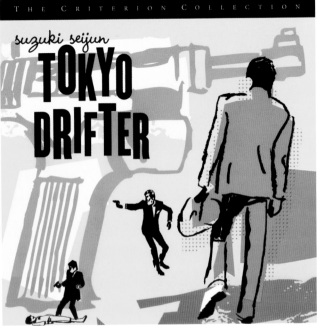

Nicoletta Ceccoli

1973 born in San Marino | lives and works in San Marino
www.nicolettaceccoli.com

"My illustrations play with contradictions. They are whimsical, but also disturbing, dreamlike and thought-provoking. Like the dark side of a nursery rhyme, a dream of lovely things with a hint of darkness."

„Meine Illustrationen spielen mit Widersprüchen. Sie sind skurril, aber auch verstörend, träumerisch und stimmen nachdenklich. Wie die dunkle Seite eines Kinderverses, wie ein Traum von liebreizenden Dingen mit einem Hauch von Dunkelheit."

« Mes illustrations jouent avec les contradictions. Elles sont fantasques, mais aussi dérangeantes et oniriques, et poussent à la réflexion. Comme le côté obscur d'une comptine, un rêve de jolies choses avec une touche ténébreuse. »

↑ Contrary Mary, 2010, Soleil, label Venusdea, *Beautiful Nightmares* art book collection, Art Direction: Barbara Canepa; acrylics on paper

→→ Hide and Seek, 2010, Soleil, label Venusdea, *Beautiful Nightmares* art book collection, Art Direction: Barbara Canepa; acrylics on paper

↑　The Magician's Assistant, 2010, Soleil,
label Venusdea, *Beautiful Nightmares*
art book collection, Art Direction:
Barbara Canepa; acrylics on paper

→　Evidently Goldfish, 2010, Soleil,
label Venusdea, *Beautiful Nightmares*
art book collection, Art Direction:
Barbara Canepa; acrylics on paper

→→　Sheryl, 2010, Soleil, label Venusdea,
Beautiful Nightmares art book collection,
Art Direction: Barbara Canepa; acrylics
on paper and Adobe Photoshop

Alonso Dubón Concha

1964 born in Valencia, Spain | lives and works in Valencia, Spain

AGENT
Smart Magna
Berlin
www.smartmagna.com

EXHIBITIONS
1. Artitude Gallery,
Paris

2. House of Valencia,
Paris

3. PSPV Gallery,
Valencia

4. Fine Arts Gallery,
Valencia

5. Ceu San Pablo,
Valencia

"My work focuses on the human figure and portraits. I use a realistic style, but very personal, with a touch of fantasy."

„In meiner Arbeit konzentriere ich mich auf die menschliche Figur und auf Porträts. Mein Stil ist realistisch, aber sehr persönlich und mit einer fantasievollen Note."

« Mon travail se centre sur la figure humaine et les portraits. Mon style est réaliste mais très personnel, avec une touche de fantaisie. »

↑   Basquiat, 2009, PSPV Gallery,
Valencia, exhibition; oil on canvas

→   Braid, 2008, Fine Arts Gallery,
Valencia, exhibition; oil on canvas

→→ Ana, 2008, Fine Arts Gallery,
Valencia, exhibition; oil on canvas

Antoine Corbineau

1982 born in Suresnes, France | lives and works in Paris, France
www.antoinecorbineau.com

AGENT
Folio Art
London
www.folioart.co.uk

EXHIBITIONS
1. Salon de Montrouge, Paris, 2011

2. Galerie Memmi, Paris, 2010

3. Illustrative, Berlin, 2009

4. "Nice Old Bank in the Corner", Apart Gallery, London, 2009

5. "Love Will Bring Us Apart", Apart Gallery, Los Angeles, 2008

"I aim to create colourful and strikingly complex illustrations."

„Mein Ziel sind farbenprächtige und eindrucksvoll komplexe Illustrationen."

« Mon but est de créer des illustrations riches en couleurs et extrêmement complexes. »

↑   Alfa Romeo 100th Anniversary Art Collection, 2011, Alfa Romeo; mixed media

→→ "Posters for Tomorrow", WWF, 2009, exhibition; mixed media

↑ Beastness, 2010, David Jaclin,
book cover illustration; mixed media

→ Underground Railroad, 2010,
One Little Indian; mixed media

←← Melbourne Public Restaurant,
2011, Darcy Group; mixed digital
printed on canvas

Augusto Costanzo

1969 born in Buenos Aires, Argentina | lives and works in Buenos Aires, Argentina
www.costhanzo.com

"I always try to create a marriage between a good synthesis of the character and its image, and a solid idea, no matter how simple it is."

„Ich versuche immer, eine grundsolide Idee, egal wie einfach sie ist, mit einer guten Darstellung des Charakters und seines Bildes zu vermählen."

«Je tente toujours de marier une bonne synthèse du personnage et de son image d'une part, et une idée solide d'autre part, aussi simple soit-elle. »

↑   Tolstoi, 2010, *Clarín* magazine;
Adobe Illustrator

→   Twitter Attack, 2010, *Página 12*
newspaper; Adobe Illustrator

→→ PencilIpod, 2009, personal work,
Adobe Illustrator

Molly Crabapple

1983 born in New York (NY), USA | lives and works in New York (NY), USA
www.mollycrabapple.com

AGENT
The Gernert Company
New York
www.thegernertco.com

EXHIBITIONS
1. "INLE", Gallery 1988, Los Angeles, 2011
2. "ReForm School", curated by Yosi Sargent, New York, 2010
3. "Politics", Museum of Sex, New York, 2010
4. "Son of Baby Tattooville", Riverside Art Museum, 2009
5. "GenArt Vanguard", Art Basel Miami, 2008

"My work is a hyper-detailed, Victorian-inspired meditation on sex, ambition, and artifice. With lots of curly lines."

„Meine Arbeit ist eine höchst detaillierte Meditation über Sex, Ehrgeiz und Kunstfertigkeit, inspiriert aus der viktorianischen Zeit. Und mit vielen verschnörkelten Linien."

« Mon travail est une réflexion très détaillée sur le sexe, l'ambition et l'artifice avec une influence victorienne et beaucoup de courbes. »

↑ The Hanged Man, 2009, Amanda Palmer, Tarot card; pen, ink and digital

→ MoCCA Art Festival, 2009, Museum of Comic and Cartoon Art, poster; pen, ink and digital

→→ Untitled, 2009, *Zupi* magazine, cover; pen, ink and digital

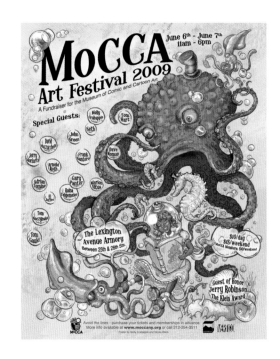

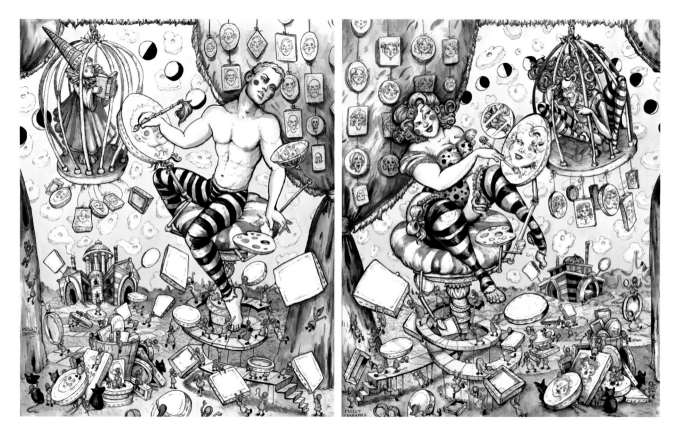

↑   Dorian Deconstructed #1 and #2,
2007, personal work, exhibition; pen,
ink, gouache and digital

→→ Octopus Girl, 2010, personal work,
exhibition; pen, ink and digital

Anne Cresci

1976 born in Loire, France | lives and works in Lyon, France

AGENT
Colagene
Paris, London, Montreal
www.colagene.com

EXHIBITIONS
1. Pin-Up exhibition,
Montreal, 2011

2. "Get Your Illustration
Fix", group show, Colagene,
Montreal and Paris, 2011

3. SkyDoll Tribute,
Gallery Nana, Paris, 2010

4. Gallery Nucleus,
Alhambra (CA), 2010

*"My work is kind of like a dream in which happiness and
melancholia get mixed up. It's full of female figures,
flowers, animals and many hidden details."*

*„Meine Arbeit ähnelt ein wenig einem Traum, in dem sich Glückseligkeit
und Melancholie miteinander mischen. Sie steckt voller weiblicher
Figuren, Blumen, Tiere und vieler verborgener Details."*

*« Mon travail ressemble à un rêve dans lequel se mêlent bonheur
et mélancolie. Il est rempli de figures féminines, de fleurs,
d'animaux et de détails cachés. »*

↑   Untitled, 2011, *BE* magazine,
editorial; Wacom tablet, Adobe
Photoshop, watercolour

→→ Get Your Illustration Fix, 2011,
Colagene, exhibition; Wacom tablet,
Adobe Photoshop, watercolour

Orlando Cuéllar

1969 born in Bogotá, Colombia | lives and works in Bogotá, Colombia
www.ocuellar.com

EXHIBITIONS

1. "There is More Than
One Truth", Go Gallery,
Amsterdam, 2010

2. "Romanticasos",
Metropolitan Center of
Design, Buenos Aires, 2010

3. "Rastreando Rostros",
Bogotá International
Book Fair, 2009

4. "Salsa Pa Vé",
Bogotá International
Book Fair, 2008

5. "Colombian Comics
and Caricature", Chapalita
Cultural Center,
Guadalajara, 2007

*"I define my illustration as an
approach or as a response to
an approach, as an opportunity
to go beyond the purely aesthetic
or decorative presence."*

„*Ich definiere meine Illustrationen
als Annäherung oder die Reaktion
auf eine Annäherung, als Chance,
um die rein ästhetische oder dekorative
Präsenz zu überwinden.*"

«*Je définis mon style d'illustration
comme une approche ou comme une
réponse à une approche, comme l'occasion
de dépasser la présence purement
esthétique ou décorative.*»

↑ Untitled, 2011, personal work;
acrylic on board

→ Alert, Scam Sighting!, 2003,
Enlaces magazine; acrylic on board

→→ Diez Lágrimas, 2007, personal work,
"Salsa Pa Vé" group exhibition;
acrylic on board

→→ Pablo Picasso, 2001, personal work,
"Rastreando Rostros" exhibition;
acrylic on board

←   Woody Allen, 2002, personal work,
"Rastreando Rostros" exhibition;
acrylic on board

↓   Untitled, 2002, VJMovement.com
website; acrylic on board

Owen Davey

1987 born in Brighton, United Kingdom | lives and works in Brighton, United Kingdom
www.owendavey.com

AGENT
Folio Art
London
www.folioart.co.uk

EXHIBITIONS
1. "Foxly's Feast", solo
show, London, 2010

2. "If in Doubt, Make Tea",
solo show, Here & Now
Gallery, Falmouth, 2010

3. "30 Years of Templar
Publishing", The Illustration
Cupboard, London, 2010

← Into The Murky Water, 2011,
Full Time Hobby, advertising; digital

→→ The Perfect Wine, 2010, *Waitrose*
magazine; digital

"My aim is to use colour, texture and pattern to create fun and entertaining images, perfect for engaging audiences in a friendly and informative manner."

„Ich setze Farben, Texturen und Muster ein, um damit lustige, unterhaltsame Bilder zu schaffen, mit denen sich der Betrachter perfekt auf freundliche und informative Weise beschäftigen kann."

« Mon but est de me servir des couleurs, des textures et des motifs pour créer des images ludiques, parfaites pour plaire au public et l'informer. »

Agnès Decourchelle

1978 born in Pessac, France | lives and works in Paris, France
http://agnesdecourchelle.blogspot.com

AGENT 1
Agent 002
Paris
www.agent002.com

AGENT 2
Eye Candy Illustration
London
www.eyecandy.co.uk

EXHIBITIONS
1. "Folio Society Prize",
Royal College of Art,
London

2. "Reading Room",
Royal College of Art,
London

"I always try to find pleasure in everything I draw. Working with light is what I enjoy the most, whether it's in colour or black and white."

„Mir ist immer daran gelegen, dass alles, was ich zeichne, für mich die reine Freude ist. Am liebsten arbeite ich mit Licht, egal ob in Farbe oder in schwarz-weißen Arbeiten."

«J'essaye toujours de trouver du plaisir dans ce que je dessine. Ce que je préfère, c'est jouer avec la lumière, que ce soit en couleur ou en noir et blanc.»

↑　L'Histoire de Kati, 2010,
Gallimard Jeunesse, book cover;
watercolour and pastels

→→　Untitled, 2007, Mucho / Carolina
Herrera, book, Art Direction: Marc Catala
& Pablo Juncadella (Mucho); mixed media

↑　Untitled, 2005, *The Observer*
newspaper, Art Direction: Marc Catala &
Pablo Juncadella (Mucho); mixed media

→→　Untitled, 2010, *Fah Thai* magazine
cover; watercolour and pencils

↓　Untitled, 2004, *Intersection* magazine,
Art Direction: Yorgo Tloupas; mixed media

Philip Dennis

1983 born in London, United Kingdom | lives and works in London, United Kingdom
www.philipdennisart.com

*"My illustration is inspired by patterns, textures,
colours and the natural world."*

*„Meine Illustrationen werden durch Muster inspiriert,
durch Oberflächenbeschaffenheit, Farben
und die Welt der Natur."*

*« Mes illustrations s'inspirent de motifs,
de textures, de couleurs et de la nature. »*

↑   Portrait of the band Warpaint,
2010, *Spindle* magazine; pencil and
Adobe Photoshop

→→ Interface, 2009, personal work;
acrylic painting and Adobe Photoshop

↑   Portrait of the band The Archie
Bronson Outfit, 2011, *Spindle* magazine;
acrylic painting and Adobe Photoshop

→   "Run, Escape", 2009, personal work;
acrylic painting, mixed media and
Adobe Photoshop

↑   1987 Playlist, 2010, *Arthur and Albert*
magazine; pencil and Adobe Photoshop

→   How To Maximise Free Audio
Software, 2011, *Wired* magazine;
pencil and Adobe Photoshop

Chris Dent

1984 born in Harlow, United Kingdom | lives and works in London, United Kingdom
www.chrisdent.co.uk

AGENT 1
Art Department
New York
www.art-dept.com

AGENT 2
Higginson Hurst
New York
www.higginsonhurst.com

AGENT 3
Serlin Associates
Paris
www.serlinassociates.com

EXHIBITIONS
1. "Pick Me Up",
Somerset House,
London, 2011

2. Christies Multiplied,
London, 2010

3. Blisters Blackout,
London, 2010

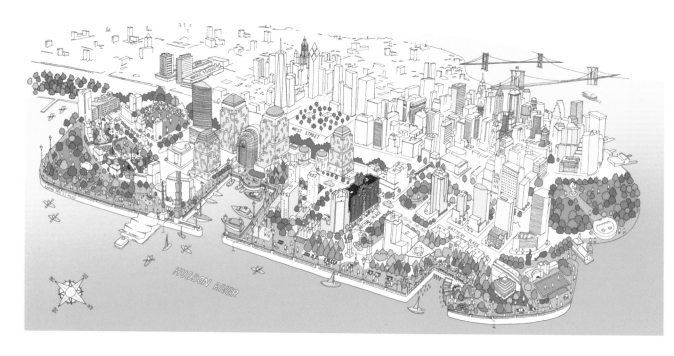

*"The original and densely informative drawings
combine reality and an original point
of view to create engaging and charming
impressions of the world."*

*„Die ursprünglichen und dicht gepackten, informativen
Zeichnungen kombinieren Realität und originelle
Standpunkte, um fesselnde und bezaubernde
Impressionen der Welt zu schaffen."*

*« Les dessins originaux et riches en informations
combinent la réalité et un point de vue
unique pour donner des impressions
agréables et attirantes sur le monde. »*

↑   Battery Park City, 2010, Rector Place,
AOL Artists; hand-drawing

→→ NY, 2009, *Vogue* magazine, USA;
hand-drawing

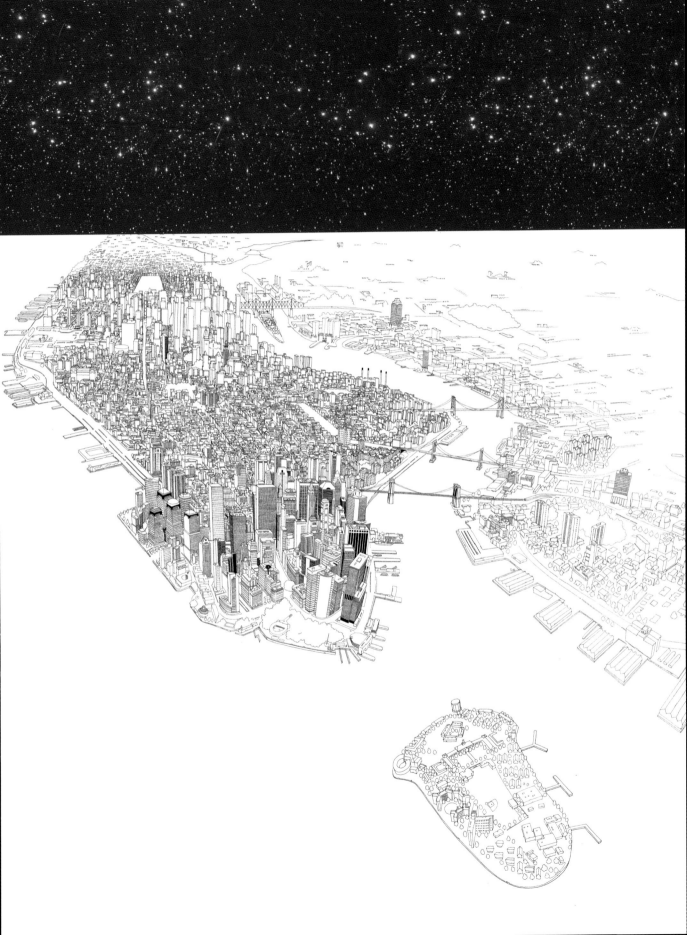

Peter Diamond

1981 born in Oxford, United Kingdom | lives and works in Vienna, Austria and in Halifax (NS), Canada
www.peterdiamond.ca

EXHIBITIONS

1. "The Deeper We Fall, The Stronger We Stay", Swoon Fine Arts, Hammonds Plains, 2011

2. "The Devils I Know", solo show, Argyle Fine Arts, Halifax, 2009

3. "An Eye for an Ear", solo show, Utility Gallery, Halifax, 2009

4. "Go North!", Studio and Gallery Tour, Halifax, 2008

5. "In the Pulp", comics show, The Rock Garden, Halifax, 2007

↑ A Dream of a Killing, 2010, personal work; India ink, alcohol ink, digital colour

→ Both Our Houses, 2010, personal work; India ink, alcohol ink, digital colour

→→ La Plongeuse et les Chauves-Patates, 2010, personal work; India ink, alcohol ink, digital colour

"Visual short stories interrupted at a point of climax. Bright colours forced into dark schemes, detailing familiar things in obscure circumstances."

„Visuelle Short Storys, unterbrochen an einem bestimmten Höhepunkt. Leuchtende Farben, die zu dunklen Machenschaften gezwungen werden, bei denen sie ausführlich von vertrauten Dingen unter obskuren Umständen erzählen."

« Des histoires courtes figées à un point culminant. Des couleurs vives intégrées à des compositions sombres, représentant des choses familières dans des circonstances obscures. »

→→ Maol, 2010, personal work;
India ink, alcohol ink, digital colour

← Stopper, 2010, personal work;
India ink, alcohol ink, digital colour

→ Shooter, 2010, personal work;
India ink, alcohol ink, digital colour

→→ The Hand-Me-Down, 2010,
personal work; India ink,
alcohol ink, digital colour

Daniel Egnéus

1972 born in Falköping, Sweden | lives and works in Milan, Italy
www.danielegneus.com

AGENT 1
Agent 002
Paris
www.agent002.com

AGENT 2
Traffic Creative
New York
www.trafficnyc.com

AGENT 3
Good Illustration
London
goodillustration.com

EXHIBITIONS
1. Red Riding Hood, solo show, Traffic Art Space, New York, 2011

2. Palazzo Bontadosi, solo show, Montefalco, 2010

3. Art Live Act, solo show, Art Basel Miami, 2009

"I see everyday life and art as one inseparable whole. My work is an expression of my colourful life in Milan and Rome and my daydreaming."

„Für mich sind alltägliches Leben und Kunst ein untrennbares Ganzes. Meine Arbeiten sind Ausdruck meines farbenprächtigen Lebens in Mailand und Rom und auch meiner Tagträumereien."

« Pour moi, le quotidien et l'art ne font qu'un. Mon travail est l'expression de ma vie colorée à Milan et à Rome et de mes rêves éveillés. »

↑ Cancro, 2010, *Velvet* magazine; watercolour, ink

→ Woman, 2011, personal work; watercolour, ink

→→ Girl, 2011, personal work; watercolour, ink

↑   Red Riding Hood III, 2010,
Harper Collins publisher, book;
watercolour, ink

←← Red Riding Hood II, 2010,
Harper Collins publisher, book;
watercolour, ink

↑ Leaving Home I, 2010,
Also Available Architecture,
animated short film;
watercolour, ink

→ Leaving Home II, 2010,
Also Available Architecture,
animated short film;
watercolour, ink

Damien "Elroy" Vignaux

1982 born in Lavelanet, France | lives and works in Berlin, Germany

AGENT
Colagene
Paris, London, Montreal
www.colagene.com

EXHIBITIONS
1. "PLAYground",
GHP Gallery,
Toulouse, 2009

2. "Elroy", solo show,
Rice and Beans Gallery,
Toulouse, 2008

3. Intoxicated Demons
Gallery, group show,
Berlin, 2007

4. "Elroy vs. Neopen",
Les Picturalistes Gallery,
Lyon, 2007

5. "Elroy vs. Neopen",
Nike Concept Store,
Warsaw, 2007

"I am influenced by pop culture, music and films, and experiment with them in a variety of media and mixed aesthetics in search of a timeless quality."

„Meine Einflüsse stammen aus Popkultur, Musik und Film. Ich experimentiere damit in verschiedenen Medien und vermische Ästhetik auf der Suche nach zeitloser Qualität."

« Je suis influencé par la culture pop, la musique et les films, et je fais des essais avec différents supports et mélanges esthétiques en quête d'une qualité intemporelle. »

↑ Get Your Illustration Fix, 2010, Colagene,
postcard; collage and Adobe Photoshop

→→ Untitled, 2009, *CNRS* newspaper;
collage and Adobe Photoshop

↑ Wlada, 2010, Vue d'Ailleurs, greetings card; collage and Adobe Photoshop

→ Untitled, 2009, *CNRS* newspaper; collage and Adobe Photoshop

↑　"Trop glamour #1, #2, #3",
2007, personal work; collage
and Adobe Photoshop

Ellen van Engelen

1979 born in Antwerp, Belgium | lives and works in Borgerhout , Belgium
www.ellenvanengelen.be

AGENT 1
Agent 002
Paris
www.agent002.com

AGENT 2
Pazuzu
Antwerp
www.pazuzu.be

"My work is in general quite feminine, but I also try to strive for something funny."

„Meine Arbeit ist generell recht feminin, aber ich achte auch darauf, etwas Lustiges einzubauen."

« Mon travail est généralement plutôt féminin, mais j'aspire aussi à ce qu'il soit amusant. »

↑ Ladies at the Movies #1, 2011, Kinepolis, advertising; pen, ink and digital

→→ Science & Kissing, 2010, *De Standaard* magazine; pen, ink and digital

↑   Ladies at the Movies #2, 2011,
Kinepolis, advertising; pen, ink
and digital

←   Strand, 2010, personal work;
pen, ink and digital

→→ Spring Fever, 2010, *De Standaard*
magazine; pen, ink and digital

Monika Fauler

1973 born in Sigmaringen, Germany | lives and works in Vienna, Austria
www.monikafauler.net

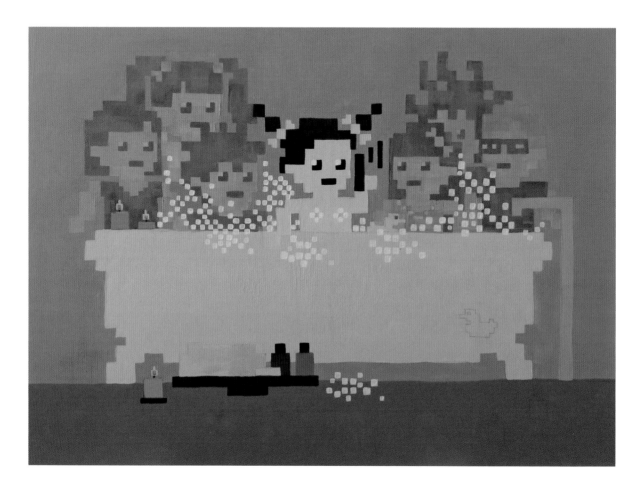

*"My artworks are experimental research into digital
and analogue worlds as well as their interrelationship
and influence on each other."*

*„In meiner künstlerischen Arbeit erforsche ich experimentell
digitale und analoge Welten, wie sie miteinander in Beziehung
stehen und sich gegenseitig beeinflussen."*

*«Mes œuvres montrent une recherche expérimentale
dans les mondes numérique et analogique, ainsi que
leur relation et leur influence mutuelle.»*

↑   Living in the Net, 2010,
Fünfwerken Design; acrylic on canvas

→→ Little Computer People, 2010,
personal work; acrylic on canvas

Rodrigo Fernandez

1976 born in Mar del Plata, Argentina | lives and works in Mar del Plata, Argentina
www.myspace.com/visionterminal

"*I try to make my work provoke an emotional reaction in the viewer. My style is surreal, dark, melancholic.*"

„*In meiner Arbeit will ich im Betrachter möglichst emotionale Reaktionen hervorrufen. Mein Stil ist surreal, dunkel, melancholisch.*"

«*Je veux que mon travail provoque une réaction émotionnelle chez le spectateur. Mon style est surréaliste, sombre et mélancolique.* »

↑   A lo que no estare invitado, 2011, personal work, book cover; mixed media, hand-painting, 3D and photography

→   Con la sombra de tus petalos, 2010, personal work, book cover; mixed media, hand-painting, 3D and photography

→→ Por que tu ansiedad, 2009, personal work, poster; mixed media, hand-painting, 3D and photography

Jesse Fillingham

1986 born in Los Angeles (CA), USA | lives and works in Pasadena (CA), USA
www.jessefillingham.com

"I am interested in fantastical worlds, non-existent creatures, escapism, fluorescent colors, tension, mythology, and rituals of the past."

„Mich interessieren fantastische Welten, nicht existente Kreaturen, Eskapismus, fluoreszierende Farben, Spannung, Mythologie und Rituale der Vergangenheit."

« Je suis attiré par les mondes fantastiques, les créatures imaginaires, l'évasion, les couleurs fluorescentes, la tension, la mythologie et les rituels du passé. »

↑ Harvest, 2010, personal work, exhibition; mixed media

→ Struggle, 2010, personal work; mixed media

→→ Clearcut, 2010, personal work; mixed media, Adobe Photoshop

David Foldvari

1973 born in Budapest, Hungary | lives and works in London, United Kingdom
www.davidfoldvari.co.uk

AGENT
Big Active
London
www.bigactive.com

EXHIBITIONS
1. Outsiders Gallery, London, 2010

2. Outline Editions, London, 2010

3. "Magma", solo show, London, 2006

4. GMW Osaka, 2004

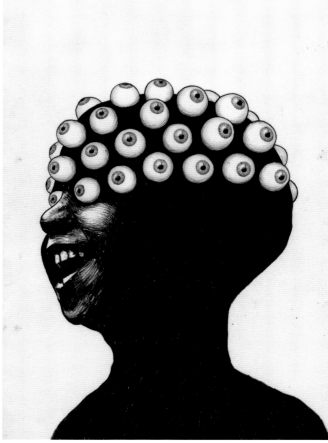

"I say what I see."

„Ich sage, was ich sehe."

« Je dis ce que je vois. »

↑   Eyeface #3, 2010, personal work, exhibition; mixed media

→   Cubik, 2010, The Room; mixed media

→→ Spring, 2011, personal work; mixed media

Gianluca Folì

1978 born in Marino, Italy | lives and works in Monte Porzio Catone and in Rome, Italy
www.gianlucafoli.com

AGENT 1
Anna Goodson
Canada
www.agoodson.com

AGENT 2
Pencil Ilustradores
Spain
www.pencil-ilustradores.com

"Feel all the mental concentration preceding the creative act which is palpable in the suspended lines and big white spaces."

„Fühle die ganze mentale Konzentration, die dem kreativen Akt vorausgeht und in unterbrochenen Linien und großen weißen Leerräumen spürbar wird."

« Sentez la concentration mentale qui précède l'acte de création, palpable dans les lignes suspendues et les grands espaces vides. »

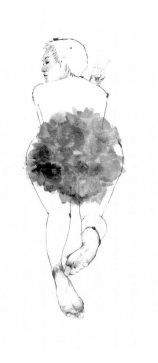

↑ Marcela Serrano – Dieci Donne, 2010, Feltrinelli, book cover; hand-drawing, crayon, watercolour, Adobe Photoshop

→ Origami Girls – Serie F, 2010, personal work; hand-drawing, ink, watercolour, Adobe Photoshop

→→ Ali Smith – La Prima Persona, 2008, Feltrinelli, book cover; pencil, watercolour, Adobe Photoshop

Bella Foster

1975 born in Los Angeles (CA), USA | lives and works in Los Angeles (CA), USA
www.bellafoster.com

AGENT
Art Department
New York
www.art-dept.com

EXHIBITIONS

1. "Interior", Art Since the Summer of '69 Gallery, New York, 2010

2. "Objects, Furniture, and Patterns", Art Since the Summer of '69, New York, 2009

3. "Still Life", Southfirst Gallery, Brooklyn, 2008

4. "Girls Gone Wild", curated by Katherine Bernhardt, Bronwyn Keenan, New York, 2003

5. "The Kids are Alright", curated by Joe Bradley, ATM Gallery, New York, 2003

"I like to embrace mistakes and the surprises that come from mistakes while making paintings. I can never predict when a good mistake is going to happen."

„Wenn ich meine Bilder male, begrüße ich die Überraschungen, die sie mit sich bringen. Ich kann nie vorhersagen, wann ein guter Fehler passiert."

« J'aime les erreurs et les surprises qui en découlent pendant que je peins. Je ne peux jamais savoir quand une bonne erreur va arriver. »

← Sunflower, 2009, personal work; watercolour

→→ Untitled, 2009, personal work; watercolour

Alejandro Fuentes

1975 born in Los Angeles (CA), USA | lives and works in Los Angeles (CA), USA
www.losfokos.com

AGENT
Illustration Ltd
New Jersey,
www.illustrationweb.com

*"My artwork is somewhat derived from comic books spiced up,
like confetti, with a dash of surrealism. I try and keep
it fluid, colorful and full of impact."*

*„Meine Kunst leitet sich gewissermaßen von aufgepeppten Comics ab – wie Konfetti
und mit einer Prise Surrealismus. Ich versuche, alles flüssig, farbig
und wirkungsvoll zu halten."*

*« Mes créations s'inspirent un peu des BD, épicées d'une touche de surréalisme,
comme des confettis. J'essaie de faire en sorte que l'ensemble soit
fluide, riche en couleurs et impactant. »*

↑ Miles, 2009, personal work;
hand-drawing, ink and Adobe Photoshop

→→ Mandrill, 2008, Teefury;
hand-drawing, graphite, acrylic
and Adobe Photoshop

Dan Goldman

1974 born in Detroit (MI), USA | lives and works in São Paulo, Brazil and in Brooklyn (NY), USA
http://dangoldman.net

EXHIBITIONS

1. Pixel Show 2010, Fecomercio, São Paulo

2. "3M Digital Show", McKenzie University, São Paulo, 2010

3. "The Art of Webcomics", Museum of Cartoon and Comic Art, New York, 2008

"I employ vector illustration, digital painting, 3D modelling and collage to build visual narratives into hyper-real and media-saturated landscapes."

„Ich arbeite mit Vektorillustrationen, digitaler Malerei, 3-D-Modellen und Collagen, um visuelle Geschichten in hyperreale Landschaften mit unterschiedlichsten Medien zu verwandeln."

« Je me sers d'illustrations vectorielles, de peinture numérique, de modèles en 3D et de collages pour construire des histoires visuelles dans des paysages hyperréalistes et saturés. »

↑ Transmetropolitan: I Hate it Here, 2011, Comic Book Legal Defense Fund; collage, Adobe Photoshop and Adobe Illustrator

→→ Black Fire, 2011, Red Light Properties, poster; Adobe Illustrator

Melissa González

1985 born in Panama | lives and works in Panama and in Buenos Aires, Argentina
http://subversivelulu.blogspot.com

"I love to use colour in the boldest way possible and capture the soul of what inspires me. Colour makes all the difference."

„Ich liebe es, Farben auf möglichst mutige Weise zu nutzen und damit die Seele dessen einzufangen, was mich inspiriert. Die Farbe sorgt für den Unterschied."

« J'aime employer la couleur avec autant d'audace que possible et capturer l'essence de ce qui m'inspire. La couleur fait toute la différence. »

↑   Juliet, 2011, personal work;
Chinese ink, acrylic, pen, mixed media

→   Girl Power, 2011, personal work;
Chinese ink, acrylic, pen, mixed media

→→ Blogger, 2011, personal work;
Chinese ink, acrylic, pen, mixed media

Luis Grañena

1968 born in Zaragoza, Spain | lives and works in Zaragoza and in Valderrobres, Spain
www.seiscuatro.com

AGENT
Illustrissimo
Paris
www.illustrissmo.com

"I try to capture the essence of people with the fewest possible elements, maintaining the expression and keeping it all clean."

„Ich versuche, das Wesen der Menschen mit möglichst wenigen Elementen einzufangen. Dabei bewahre ich den Ausdruck und halte alles klar und aufgeräumt."

« Je tente de saisir l'essence des personnes avec le moins d'éléments possible, en conservant l'expression et en évitant toute surcharge. »

↑   Karl Lagerfeld, 2010, *Libération* newspaper,
Art Direction: Alain Blaise; Adobe Freehand,
Adobe Photoshop

→   Michael Jackson, 2009, *Sábado* newspaper,
Art Direction: Fernando Barata; Adobe Freehand,
Adobe Photoshop

→→ Marilyn, 2010, *Heraldo de Aragón* newspaper,
Art Direction: Cristina Urresti; Adobe Freehand,
Adobe Photoshop

Nazario Graziano

1975 born in Campobasso, Italy | lives and works in Ancona, Italy

AGENT
Colagene
Paris, London, Montreal
www.colagene.com

EXHIBITIONS
1. Konen/Bram Store, solo show, Munich and Luxembourg, 2011

2. Genuine Roman Art, Rome, 2008

3. Big Babel, solo show, Campobasso, 2006

4. Gemine Muse, Campobasso, 2005

5. Art Trek, Antwerp, 2005

"A romantic outlook, tinged with a bit of irony."

„Eine romantische Anschauung, gefärbt mit einem Schuss Ironie."

« Une perspective romantique, teintée d'une dose d'ironie. »

↑   Untitled, 2011, *Premiere* magazine; mixed media

→   Untitled, 2011, Toxic.fm, advertising; mixed media

→→ Untitled, 2011, *Bulletin* magazine; mixed media

↑   Untitled, 2010, *The Sunday Times* newspaper; mixed media

→   Untitled, 2011, *Philosophie* magazine; mixed media

→ Untitled, 2011, *Philosophie*
magazine; mixed media

↓ Untitled, 2010, personal work,
poster; mixed media

Cyril "Guru" Garant

1968 born in Sedan, France | lives and works in Aiglemont, France
www.monsieurbuzz.fr

EXHIBITIONS

1. Pèze & Cash, Pézénas, 2011

2. Born Bad, Paris, 2008

3. La Cartonnerie, Reims, 2007

4. Sedan's City Media, 2006

"From a poster, a movie or a situation based on the collective consciousness, I 'cartoonise' everything I touch, in a retro, vintage '50s and '60s style."

„Ausgehend von einem Plakat, einem Film oder einer Situation, die auf dem kollektiven Unbewussten gründet, verwandle ich alles, was ich anfasse, in cartoonähnliche Szenerien im Stil der 50er- und 60er-Jahre."

«À partir d'une affiche, d'un film ou d'une situation partant de la conscience collective, je ‹cartoonifie› tout ce que je touche dans un style rétro et vintage des années 1950-60.»

↑   Faster Pussycat! Buzz! Buzz!, 2011, Buzz Buzz, advertising; Adobe Illustrator

→   Le Fifre, 2011, Buzz Buzz; Adobe Illustrator

→→ The Creature from the Buzz Lagoon, 2006, Buzz Buzz, advertising; Adobe Illustrator

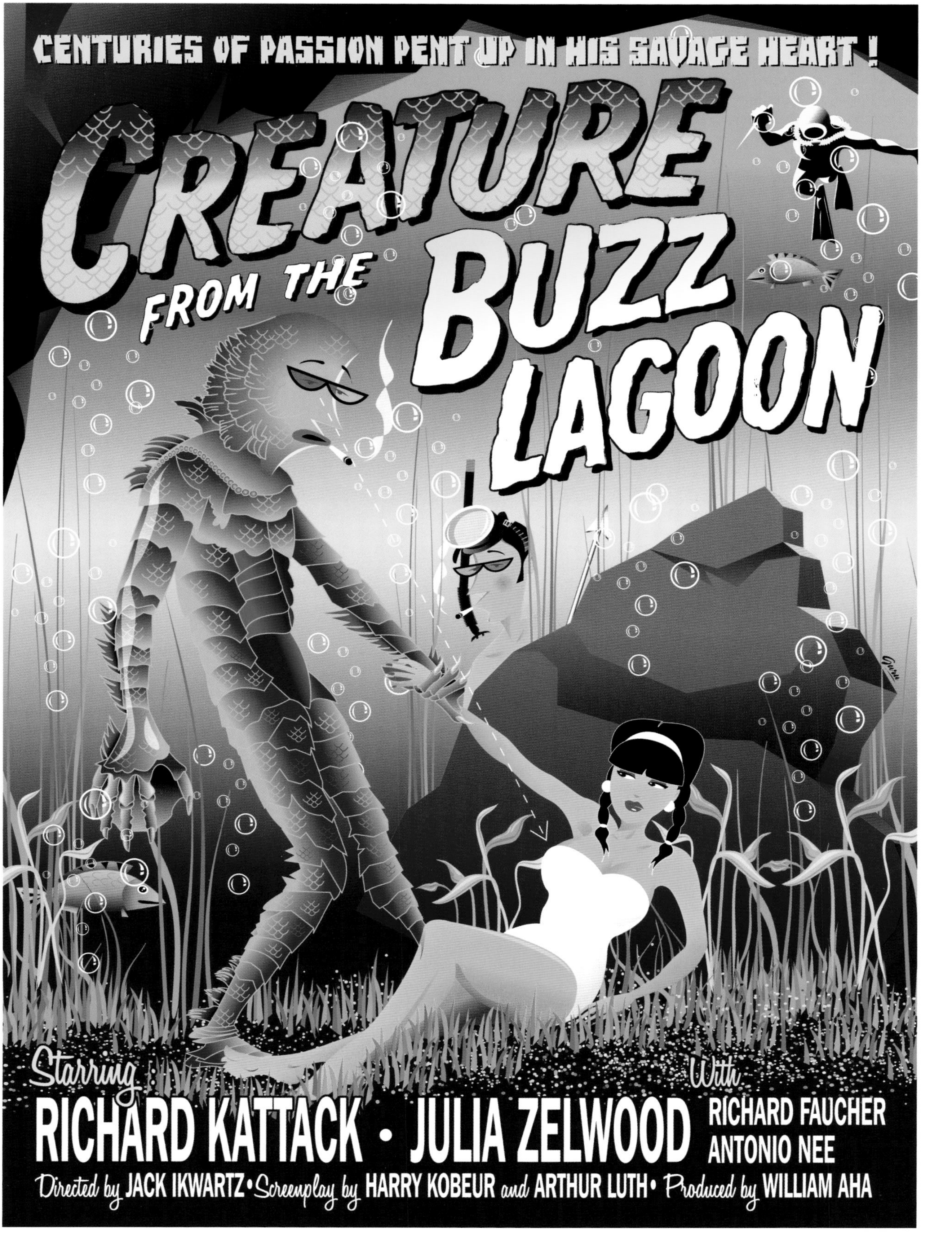
CENTURIES OF PASSION PENT UP IN HIS SAVAGE HEART !
CREATURE
FROM THE
BUZZ
LAGOON
Starring
RICHARD KATTACK • JULIA ZELWOOD
With
RICHARD FAUCHER
ANTONIO NEE
Directed by JACK IKWARTZ • Screenplay by HARRY KOBEUR and ARTHUR LUTH • Produced by WILLIAM AHA

Catarina Gushiken

1981 born in São Paulo, Brazil | lives and works in São Paulo, Brazil
www.catarinagushiken.com

*"As an illustrator I materialise my wishes,
dreams and questions. Illustrating
is one of my vital senses."*

*„Als Illustratorin lasse ich all meine Wünsche, Träume
und Fragen Gestalt annehmen. Das Illustrieren
gehört zu meinen lebenswichtigen Sinnen."*

*« En tant qu'illustratrice, je matérialise mes souhaits,
mes rêves et mes interrogations. L'illustration
est l'un de mes sens vitaux. »*

↑   Thirst, 2010, *S/N* magazine;
watercolour and India ink

→→ Múltiplos Eus, 2010, Urban Arts,
virtual gallery; watercolour, India ink
and ecoline ink

Luci Gutiérrez

1977 born in Barcelona, Spain | lives and works in Barcelona, Spain
www.holeland.com

AGENT
Kate Larkworthy
New York
www.larkworthy.com

*"I consider illustration to be more than just decoration.
I like pictures which tell me something or suggest
something, and that is the way I try to create them.
I am drawn to simplicity in beauty, something
which can say a lot using very little."*

*„Ich betrachte Illustrationen nicht als reine Dekoration. Mir gefallen Bilder,
die mir etwas sagen wollen oder mich auf Ideen bringen. Das ist auch
die Art, wie ich sie zu schaffen versuche. Mich zieht die Einfachheit in
der Schönheit an, wenn man mit sehr wenig ganz viel aussagen kann."*

*« L'illustration est pour moi bien plus qu'une décoration. J'aime les images
qui me parlent ou me suggèrent quelque chose, et c'est ainsi que j'aborde
mes créations. Je prête une attention particulière à la simplicité de la
beauté, une chose qui peut dire beaucoup avec très peu d'éléments. »*

↑   Pandora's Bed, 2009, El Mundo,
blog; hand-drawing and digital

→→ Grand Obsession, 2008,
The New York Times Book Review
magazine, Art Direction: Nicholas
Blechman; hand-drawing and digital

James Gulliver Hancock

1977 born in Sydney, Australia | lives and works in New York (NY), USA and in Sydney, Australia
www.jamesgulliverhancock.com

AGENT
Jacky Winter Group
Melbourne
http://jackywinter.com

EXHIBITIONS
1. "Visions", Sheffer Gallery, Sydney, 2011

2. "You Win", Nina Sagt Gallery, Düsseldorf, 2010

3. "We Will Not Grow Old", No. 12 Gallery, Tokyo, 2009

4. "Desiring Machines", Lamington Drive Gallery, Melbourne, 2009

5. "Thought Patterns", Space3 Gallery, Sydney, 2008

↑   Hoarders, 2010, *Hour Media* magazine; pencil, scanner and Adobe Photoshop

→   Confession, 2010, *News Ltd* magazine; pencil, scanner and Adobe Photoshop

→→ Dark Matter, 2010, *MIT Technology Review* magazine; pencil, scanner and Adobe Photoshop

"I am interested in imbuing objects and experiences with visions of whimsy and romance. My work is rooted in obsession, psychology, and philosophy."

„Ich interessiere mich dafür, Objekte und Erfahrungen mit Visionen von Launenhaftigkeit und Romantik zu durchtränken. Meine Arbeiten wurzeln in Obsessionen, Psychologie und Philosophie."

«Je cherche à imprégner les objets et les expériences de visions fantaisistes et romantiques. Mon travail trouve ses racines dans l'obsession, la psychologie et la philosophie.»

lives here...

↑ New York Man #1 and #2, 2010,
personal work; acrylic and ink on board

↑   Narrators, 2010, *Cent* magazine;
ink, collage, scanner and Adobe Photoshop

↓   Cap and Trade, 2010, *Businessweek* magazine;
ink, collage, scanner and Adobe Photoshop

Fred Harper

1967 born in Grove City (PA), USA | lives and works in New York (NY), USA
www.fredharper.com

EXHIBITIONS

1. "INLE", Gallery 1988, Los Angeles, 2011

2. Last Rites Gallery, solo show, New York, 2010

3. BK Mia show Art Basel Miami, 2009

4. La Luz de Jesus, Los Angeles, 2007

5. Art at Large Gallery, group show, Melbourne, 2005

"My work includes elements of machinery with animals, humans, and buildings to create surreal landscapes that cause the viewer to wonder what this world is."

„In meinen Arbeiten binde ich neben Tieren, Menschen und Gebäuden auch maschinelle Elemente ein, um surreale Landschaften zu kreieren. Der Betrachter wundert sich dann, was das wohl für eine Welt sein mag."

« Mon travail inclut des éléments de machinerie, des animaux, des hommes et des bâtiments pour créer des paysages surréalistes, face auxquels le spectateur se demande quel est ce monde. »

↑ Salesman, 2008, *The Week* magazine, cover; gouache on paper and digital

→ Spector, 2010, personal work; gouache on paper

→→ Terrorist, 2010, *The Week* magazine, cover; gouache on paper and digital

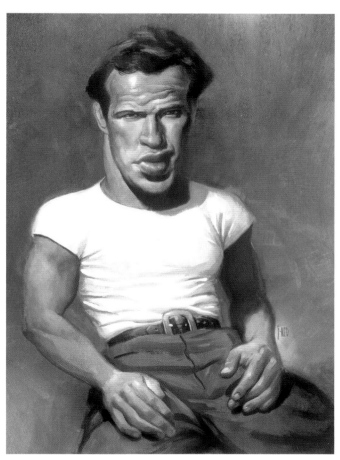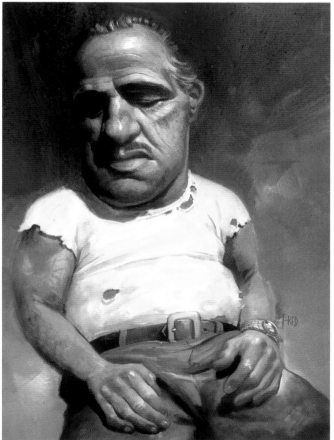

↑　"Young Brando" and "Older Brando",
2010, personal work; gouache on paper

←← No Nukes!, 2010, personal work;
gouache on paper

Minni Havas

1983 born in Lahti, Finland | lives and works in Helsinki, Finland
www.minnihavas.fi

AGENT
Pekka Finland
Helsinki
www.pekkafinland.fi

EXHIBITIONS
1. Aalto University School
of Art and Design, 140th
anniversary exhibition,
Helsinki, 2011

2. The Picture Room
of Agent Pekka, solo show,
Helsinki, 2009

*"I draw detailed pictures
somewhere in the borderlands
of the real and the imaginary."*

*„Ich zeichne detaillierte Bilder, die irgendwo
aus dem Grenzgebiet zwischen Realem
und Imaginärem stammen."*

*« Je dessine des images détaillées qui
se situent à la frontière entre
la réalité et l'imaginaire. »*

↑   Untitled, 2010, personal work;
coloured pencils and Adobe Photoshop

→   Helene 1, 2009, Anne Törnroos;
coloured pencils, acrylic, cardboard
and Adobe Photoshop

→→ Untitled, 2010, personal work;
coloured pencils, watercolours
and Adobe Photoshop

→→ Untitled, 2003, Finatex;
coloured pencils and watercolours

← Untitled, 2003, personal work;
coloured pencils

Kerrie Hess

1979 born in Brisbane, Australia | lives and works in Paris, France
www.kerriehess.com

AGENT 1
IlloReps
New York
www.illoreps.com

AGENT 1
Art Liaison
Tokyo
www.art-liaison.com

"I like to think of my work as eclectic with a fashion base. Vogue, fashion blogs, style.com and my neighbourhood in Paris are daily inspirations."

„Meine Arbeit beschreibe ich gerne als eklektisch mit einer modischen Basis. Vogue, Mode-Blogs, style.com und das Viertel von Paris, in dem ich lebe, sind meine täglichen Inspirationen."

« Je considère mon travail comme éclectique, avec des racines dans la mode. Vogue, les blogs de mode, style.com et mon quartier à Paris m'inspirent tous les jours. »

↑   Le Balmain, 2010, *InStyle* Australia, magazine; watercolour and ink

→   La Rodarte, 2010, *InStyle* Australia, magazine; watercolour and ink

→→ Perfectly Prada, 2010, *InStyle* Australia, magazine; watercolour and ink

Anna Higgie

1985 born in Canberra, Australia │ lives and works in Barcelona, Spain
www.annahiggie.com

AGENT
Art Department
New York
www.art-dept.com

*"I have always drawn, ever since I can remember,
so eventually becoming an illustrator seemed
like the most natural thing for me to do."*

*„Ich habe immer gezeichnet, solange ich denken kann.
Also war es für mich total natürlich, als ich
schließlich Illustratorin wurde."*

*« J'ai dessiné toute ma vie ; me consacrer
à l'illustration était donc pour moi
la chose la plus naturelle du monde. »*

↑　Sarah Cracknell (Saint Etienne),
2008, *Plan B* magazine; hand-drawing

→→　The Virgin Suicides, 2010, personal
work; hand-drawing and digital colour

↑　Sigerson Morrison A/W 2010,
website; hand-drawing and digital

↗　Belle NYC, 2009, Sigerson
Morrison, website; hand-drawing
and digital

→　Untitled, 2009, personal work;
hand-drawing

↑   Jamie Lidell, 2010, *Bonafide* magazine;
hand-drawing and digital

Paul Hoppe

1976 born in Biskupiec, Poland | lives and works in Brooklyn (NY), USA and in Weingarten, Germany
www.paulhoppe.com

"Whether it's an editorial illustration, a comic or a children's book, I like telling stories with drawings, and imagining locations and atmosphere."

„Ich erzähle durch Zeichnungen – egal ob als Artikelillustration, Comic oder Kinderbuch – liebend gerne Geschichten und male mir Orte und Stimmungen aus."

« Qu'il s'agisse d'une illustration pour la presse, d'une bande dessinée ou d'un livre pour enfants, j'aime raconter des histoires avec mes dessins et imaginer des lieux et des ambiances. »

↑ Los Angeles in the Future, 2011, *UCLA* magazine, cover, Art Direction: Charlie Hess; non-photo blue, ink, pencil, pen, brush and digital

→ Inspiration, 2010, *Assets* magazine of Anderson Business School at UCLA, Art Direction: Charlie Hess; pen, ink, paper and digital

→→ Rabid Rabbits over Brooklyn, 2010, exhibition; non-photo blue, ink, pencil, pen, brush and digital

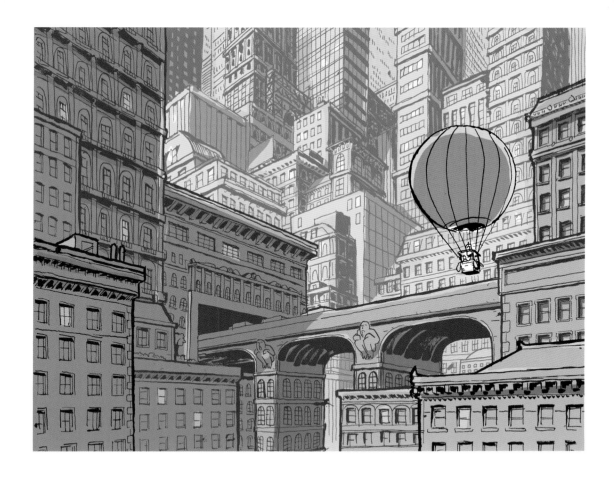

↑   Destinations, 2007, Finest/Magma
Design & Communication Group,
calendar and agenda, Art Direction:
Christopher Karl and Lars Harmsen;
non-photo blue, ink, pencil, pen,
brush and digital

←   Coney Island Sunset, 2008,
Philadelphia Weekly website and
emailing; pen, ink and digital

←← Green Line Café, 2007,
Philadelphia Weekly newspaper,
Art Direction: Sara Green; non-photo
blue, ink, pencil, pen, brush and digital

Patrick Hruby

1981 born in Los Angeles (CA), USA | lives and works in Los Angeles (CA), USA
www.patrickdrawsthings.com

AGENT
Friend + Johnson
USA
www.friendandjohnson.com

*"My work is about the celebration of color and the
precision of design. I strive to achieve beauty through
clean shape and vibrant harmonies."*

*„In meiner Arbeit feiere ich Farben und die Präzision des Designs.
Durch klare Formen und pulsierende Harmonien will ich
Schönheit erreichen."*

*« Mon travail est un hommage à la couleur et à la précision
du trait. Je m'efforce d'atteindre la beauté grâce à des formes
pures et des harmonies vibrantes. »*

↑   Imaginary Castle, 2010,
AMMO Books; Adobe Illustrator

→→   A-Frame, 2010, personal work;
Adobe Illustrator

Anne Iblings

1982 born in Bielefeld, Germany | lives and works in Dresden, Germany
www.illustrakt.de

EXHIBITIONS

1. "Hier & woanders",
Werkstattladen,
Kunsthof Dresden, 2010

2. "Seitenwege – unterwegs
in Dresden", Galerie Adam
Ziege, Dresden, 2009

*"My drawings indicate my perception of the outside world.
Paying attention to ordinary objects revives them."*

*„Meine Zeichnungen spiegeln meine Wahrnehmung der Umwelt.
Alltägliche Gegenstände werden lebendig, indem ich ihnen besondere Aufmerksamkeit schenke."*

*« Mes dessins reflètent ma perception du monde extérieur.
Le fait de porter l'attention sur des objets ordinaires les fait revivre. »*

↑   Hebedas, 2009,
Die Verlagsgesellschaft,
book; fineliner and
watercolour

←   Dächerblick, 2007,
personal work, book;
fineliner and watercolour

→→ Nasenbär, 2005,
personal work; fineliner,
colour pencils and
watercolour

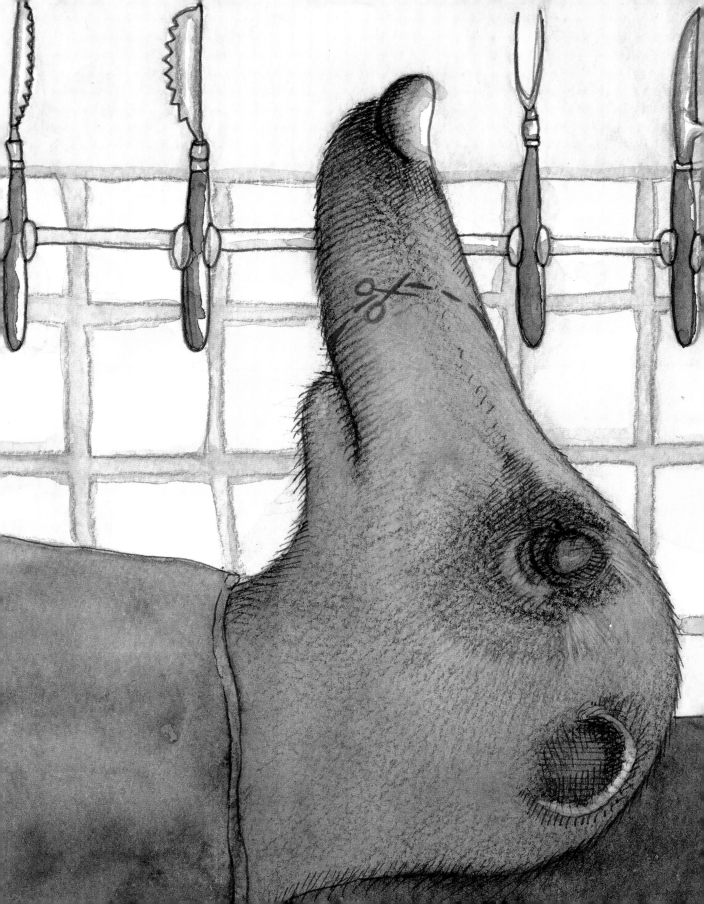

IC4Design

1998 founded | located in Hiroshima, Japan
www.ic4design.com

"*A miniature garden which we filled with feelings. The place we want to live in, we want to go to, we can enjoy, and our hope and adoration.*"

„Ein Miniaturgarten, den wir mit Gefühlen gefüllt haben. Der Ort, an dem wir leben wollen, den wir aufsuchen wollen, den wir genießen – der Ort unserer Hoffnung und Verehrung."

« Un jardin miniature rempli de sentiments. L'endroit où nous voulons vivre, où nous voulons aller, que nous pouvons aimer, nos espoirs et notre adoration. »

↑   Ginza, 2010, personal work;
Adobe Photoshop and Corel Painter

→   National Train Day, 2010,
Amtrak, poster, billboard and banner;
Adobe Photoshop and Corel Painter

→→ Micro DNA, 2009, *HHMI* magazine;
Adobe Photoshop and Corel Painter

↑   World Neverland, 2008, Alti,
online game; Adobe Photoshop
and Corel Painter

Indio San

1978 born in Santiago, Brazil | lives and works in São Paulo, Brazil
http://indiosan.com

"I believe that every project asks for its own aesthetic concept. My job is to find out and design it."

„Ich glaube, dass jedes Projekt sein eigenes ästhetisches Konzept verlangt. Mein Job besteht darin, dieses Konzept herauszufinden und es zu gestalten."

« Pour moi, chaque projet demande un concept esthétique particulier. Mon travail consiste à le trouver et à le concevoir. »

↑ The Duel: Jagger vs. Bono, 2008, *MTV* magazine; digital

→→ Rock's Birthday, 2007, *MTV* magazine; digital

← Procrastination series, 2009,
Vida Simples magazine; mixed media

→→ "Tourist" and "Fisher", 2010,
Giovanni+Draftfcb / Baygon,
magazine advertising; mixed media

Nicole Jarecz

1988 born in Mount Clemens (MI), USA | lives and works in Paris, France and in Detroit (MI), USA
www.nicolejarecz.ultra-book.com

AGENT
Colagene
Paris, London, Montreal
www.colagene.com

EXHIBITIONS
1. "Get Your Illustration
Fix", Colagene, Paris, 2010

"Delicate and feminine, created with graphite, watercolour and found textures. Inspired by fashion, travel, people-watching and living in Paris."

„Filigran und feminin, geschaffen aus Grafit, Wasserfarben und gefundenen Texturen. Inspiriert durch Mode, Reisen, Leutebeobachten und Leben in Paris."

« Créations délicates et féminines, à l'aide de graphite, d'aquarelles et de textures rencontrées, inspirées de la mode, des voyages, de l'observation des gens et de la vie à Paris. »

↑   Tongue, 2010, personal work;
graphite, Adobe Photoshop,
watercolour, collage

→   Club, 2010, personal work;
pencil, Adobe Photoshop,
watercolour, collage

→→ Ray Ban, 2010, personal work;
pencil, Adobe Photoshop,
watercolour, collage

Jean Jullien

1983 born in Cholet, France | lives and works in London, United Kingdom
www.jeanjullien.com

AGENT 1
Illustrissimo
Paris
www.illustrissimo.com

AGENT 2
YCN
London
www.ycnonline.com

EXHIBITIONS
1. "Machin Machine",
Paris

2. "The Village",
Cambridge (UK)

3. "I Judge a Book by
its Cover", Marseille

4. "Knock Knock",
Edinburgh

> *"I try to convey messages and tell stories by making people smile and/or think. I use bold colours, hand-written words and a minimal, semi-naive imagery."*

„Ich versuche, Botschaften zu vermitteln und Geschichten zu erzählen, indem ich die Menschen zum Lächeln und/oder Nachdenken bringe. Ich arbeite mit kräftigen Farben, handgeschriebenen Wörtern und einer minimalen, halb naiven Bildgestaltung."

« Je tente de transmettre des messages et de raconter des histoires en faisant rire ou réfléchir les gens. J'emploie des couleurs fortes, des textes manuscrits et une esthétique minimale et semi-naïve. »

↑ Blinds, 2011, personal work,
poster; brush pen and ink

→ Mac Book, 2011, personal work,
poster; brush pen and ink

→→ The Republic, 2010, personal work,
poster; brush pen and ink

↑ Big Chill Festival, 2009, The Big Chill,
poster, Photography: Erik Hartin;
brush pen, ink and paper

↑ La Fontaine, 2008, personal work,
poster; brush pen, ink, paper, photography

↖ LOL Gun, 2011, It's Nice that / Asos,
T-shirt; brush pen and ink

↑   Catastrophe, 2010, Niwouinwouin,
album cover; brush pen, ink, paper and
photography

Kitty Kahane

1960 born in Berlin, Germany | lives and works in Berlin, Germany
www.kitty.de

AGENT
Smart Magna
Berlin
www.smartmagna.com

EXHIBITIONS

1. "Lebensform Demokratie", solo show, Berlin and Tel Aviv, 2011

2. "Book Illustration", solo show, Frankfurt, 2011

3. Students of Volker Pfüller, Berlin, 2010

4. "The Five Senses", solo show, Berlin, 2009

5. "Diary in Pictures", solo show, Berlin, 2008

"My art includes both poetic illustrations for good literature and free-work. I see both as answers to the big issues of our times."

„Zu meiner Kunst gehören sowohl poetische Illustrationen guter Literatur als auch freie Arbeiten. Ich betrachte beides als Antworten auf die großen Themen unserer Zeit."

« Mon art inclut des illustrations poétiques pour des œuvres littéraires et des créations libres. Je considère les deux comme des réponses aux grands problèmes de notre temps. »

↑   You'll Never Walk Alone, 2008, Chrismon, book, Art Direction: Brigitte Jung; hand-drawing

→→ Das Leben ist kein Joghurt, 2010, Chrismon, book, Art Direction: Elke Rutzenhöfer; hand-drawing

Takahiro Kimura

1965 born in Tokyo, Japan | lives and works in Tokyo, Japan
www.faceful.jp

"Faces of human beings."

„*Gesichter von Menschen.*"

«*Des visages d'êtres humains.*»

↑ Red Hair, 2009, personal work; collage

→ Boy, 2008, personal work; collage

→→ Patch Dreams, 2010, personal work; collage

↑   New Arrivals, 2010, personal work; collage

↓   Shell, 2010, personal work; collage

→   Sprout, 2010, personal work; collage

↓   Green man, 2008, personal work; collage

↑ Crazy Love, 2009, personal work; collage

→→ World, 2008, personal work; collage

Evgeny Kiselev

1980 born in St. Petersburg, Russia | lives and works in St. Petersburg, Russia
www.ekiselev.com

AGENT
Satellite Office
Chicago
www.satelliteoffice.tv

EXHIBITIONS

1. Oh! Yeah! Art & Design Festival, Buenos Aires, 2011

2. Mocha Arthouse, solo show, New Delhi, 2010

3. 100 Svoih Gallery, solo show, St. Petersburg, 2008

4. Freakypeople, group show, St. Petersburg, 2006

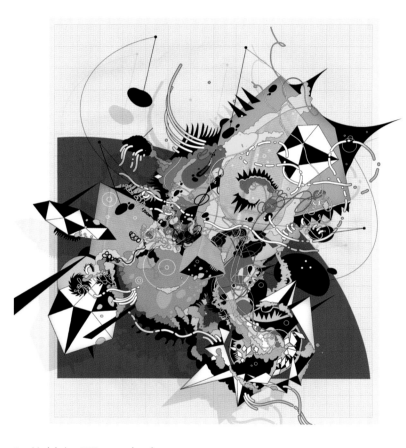

↑ Modulation, 2009, personal work; Adobe FreeHand

→ Skyscraper, 2010, personal work; Adobe FreeHand

→→ Good Point, 2007, personal work; Adobe FreeHand and Adobe Photoshop

"I strive for a complexity of colour and layers that continues to build infinitely into the space of the page creating a warping spatial depth."

„Mir ist daran gelegen, durch komplexe Farben und Schichten unendlich in den Raum des Blatts hineinzubauen und so eine gekrümmte Raumtiefe zu schaffen."

« J'aspire à une complexité de couleurs et de strates qui évolue à l'infini dans la page et crée une profondeur spatiale. »

↑ Krugovorot, 2010, personal work;
Adobe FreeHand and Adobe Photoshop

→ The City, 2010, personal work;
Adobe FreeHand

←← Indigo Kids, 2007, APAG for
UNICEF, *60 Unite for Children*, book;
Adobe FreeHand

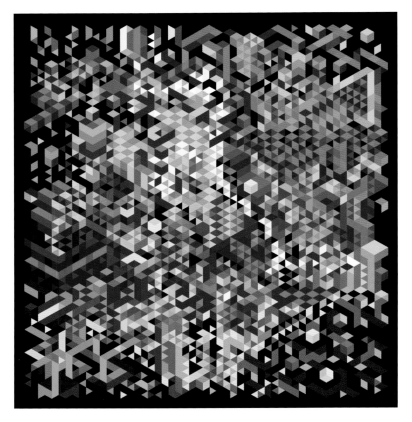

Karen Klassen

1977 born in High Level, Canada | lives and works in Calgary, Canada

AGENT
Colagene
Paris, London, Montreal
www.colagene.com

"My interest in portraiture and fashion, and mixed media impacts on everything I do in art, from how I choose subjects to ultimately how I portray that image."

„Mein Interesse für Porträts und Mode sowie Mixed Media wirkt sich auf mein gesamtes künstlerisches Handeln aus – so wähle ich meine Themen, und letzten Endes beeinflusst das auch, wie ich dieses Bild dann porträtiere."

« Mon intérêt pour les portraits, la mode et le mélange de supports influence toutes mes œuvres, du choix des sujets à ma façon de concevoir l'image finale. »

↑ Untitled, 2009, RC Lofts Chicago / Otherwise Inc; mixed media

→→ Poppy Crown, 2009, Market Mall / Zero Gravity; acrylic and oil on paper

200

↑   Lolita Series – Chris and Lola,
2010, personal work; acrylic and
oil on panel

→   Lolita Series – Amy, 2010,
personal work; acrylic and
oil on panel

←← Untitled, 2009, Colagene;
acrylic and digital

Roman Klonek

1969 born in Katowice, Poland | lives and works in Düsseldorf, Germany
www.klonek.de

AGENT
Frank Sturges
Columbus, OH
www.sturges.com

EXHIBITIONS
1. "At this Unreasonable Hour", Pictoplasma, Berlin, 2011

2. "Ratibor Knights", Galerie Kielkind, Kiel, 2010

3. "Flux Gate Kasachok", Kemistry Gallery, London, 2009

4. Comicuts, Jörg Heitsch Galerie, Munich, 2009

5. "Hobnobbing zmirkies", Gallery McCaig Welles, New York, 2008

"I have a soft spot for old-fashioned cartoons, especially East European styles."

„Ich habe ein Faible für altmodische Trickfilme, vor allem solche im osteuropäischen Stil.“

« J'ai un faible pour les vieux dessins animés, notamment ceux d'Europe de l'Est. »

↑   j_j_x_x_, 2010, personal work; woodcut

→   Ratibor, 2010, personal work; woodcut

→→   The New Power Generation, 2010, personal work; woodcut

→→ The Observer, 2011, personal work; woodcut

← Storysisters, 2010, *The New York Times* newspaper; Adobe Photoshop

↓ Mr and Mrs Markusi, 2010, personal work; woodcut

↘   Nice Try, 2010,
personal work; woodcut

↓   Hey Kids, 2010,
personal work; woodcut

Thomas Knowler

1984 born in London, United Kingdom | lives and works in London, United Kingdom and in New York (NY), USA
www.knowlerdraws.co.uk

EXHIBITIONS

1. Monstra Animation Festival 2011, Lisbon

2. Too Art 4 TV, Erebuni Gallery, Brooklyn, 2010

3. Bucharest Kinofest Animation Festival 2010

4. Alumni Scholarship Show, School of Visual Arts Gallery, New York, 2010

5. Aurora Animation Festival, Norwich, 2007

↑ Tunbridge Wells Pantiles #3, 2011, personal work; ink, pen, digital tablet, Adobe Photoshop

→ Dalton Trumbo's "Johnny Got His Gun" , 2009, book; ink, pen, digital tablet, Adobe Photoshop

→→ JG Ballard's "Drowned World" cover concept, 2011, book; ink, pen, digital tablet, Adobe Photoshop

"I try to create immersive experiences, through detailed illustration or animation, in which the viewer can explore an idea or story through drawing."

„Durch detaillierte Illustrationen oder Animationen, in denen der Betrachter durch die Zeichnungen eine Idee oder Story erforschen kann, versuche ich, eindringliche Erfahrungen zu schaffen.“

«Je tente de provoquer des expériences immersives, par le biais d'illustrations ou d'animations détaillées dans lesquelles le spectateur peut explorer une idée ou une histoire à travers le dessin.»

Anne Kobsa

1985 born in Wittenberg, Germany | lives and works in Hamburg, Germany
www.annekobsa.wordpress.com

EXHIBITIONS

1. "Der Großstadtbaum &
die Großstadtvögel", Atelier
Simpel, Hamburg, 2010

2. "Das Gesicht
Südamerikas", Atelier
Simpel, Hamburg, 2010

3. "Walsrode Exotic", Atelier
Simpel, Hamburg, 2010

4. "Fingerprints",
Kunst Kiosk, Hamburg,
2010

*"Every once in a while a new idea comes to my mind, that is
why I could never limit myself to only one picture language.
Finding a way of bringing different media to a handmade and
contemporary illustration is the challenge for me, and I love it!"*

*„Von Zeit zu Zeit fallen mir ganz neue Ideen ein, und darum könnte ich mich auch
nicht auf nur eine Bildsprache beschränken. Für mich besteht die Herausforderung darin,
unterschiedliche Medien in einer von Hand gefertigten und zeitgenössischen
Illustration zusammenzubringen, und genau das liebe ich!"*

*« De temps à autre, une nouvelle idée me vient à l'esprit, ce qui m'empêche de me limiter
à un seul langage pictural. Combiner plusieurs techniques dans une illustration
contemporaine faite à la main suppose tout un défi, chose que j'adore ! »*

↑   Wooden Being a Blockhead, 2011,
personal work; wooden bonding sheets
collage and digital

→→   Wooden Being, 2010, personal work;
wooden bonding sheets collage and digital

→→ Fingerprint Horoscope, 2010,
Bauer Women GmbH - Maxi;
my fingerprint, ink, watercolours
and coloured pencil

←   i-Robic #1, 2010, personal work;
watercolours, ink, collage

↓   i-Robic #2, 2010, personal work;
watercolours, ink, collage

Stuart Kolakovic

1985 born in Stafford, United Kingdom | lives and works in Stafford, United Kingdom
www.stuartkolakovic.co.uk

AGENT
Heart
London, New York
www.heartagency.com

EXHIBITIONS

1. "Under the Damp Earth",
Nobrow Gallery, London,
2011

2. "In 50 Comics um die
Welt", Neurotitan Gallery,
Berlin, 2010

3. "The Exquisite Book
Project", Powerhouse Arena,
New York, 2010

4. "Never Been", Projekts
MCR, Manchester,
Dec 2007–Feb 2008

5. "The Joyful
Bewilderment", Rough
Trade East, London, 2008

↑   Pension Schemes, 2010,
Employee Benefits magazine,
cover; ink and digital

→   Right On, 2010, Todryfor,
tea towel; screenprint

→→ Russia, 2009, Rotopol Press,
print; ink and digital

"My interest in illustration stems from my desire to tell stories visually. I attempt to inject a narrative into all of my drawings."

„Mein Interesse an Illustrationen wurzelt in meinem Wunsch, visuelle Geschichten zu erzählen. In allen meinen Zeichnungen versuche ich, etwas Erzählendes einzuführen."

« Mon intérêt pour l'illustration vient de mon souhait de raconter des histoires de façon visuelle. J'essaie d'introduire un aspect narratif dans tous mes dessins. »

↑ Topsy Turvy, 2010, *NoBrow* magazine;
ink, digital and lithography

↑   Autonomads LP cover, 2010,
Pumpkin Records; ink and digital

←← Marks & Spencer "Naturally Caffeine
Free Tea" boxes, 2010; ink and digital

Bartosz Kosowski

1979 born in Kolno, Poland | lives and works in Lodz, Poland
www.bartoszkosowski.com

EXHIBITIONS

1. Stripdagen –
De Kampensche School
(Nieuwe Vide), Haarlem,
2010

2. International Comic
Book Festival, solo show,
Lodz, 2008

3. "Good 50x70", Milan,
2008

4. "Ten Images for Ithaca",
2007

↑   Wojciech Smarzowski, 2009, *Przekroj*
magazine, Art Direction: Anna Mysluk;
pencil, watercolour, Adobe Photoshop

→   Agnieszka Holland, 2011,
Przekroj magazine, Art Direction:
Kasper Skirgajllo-Krajewski,
Photography: Wojciech Surdziel;
pencil, watercolour, Adobe Photoshop

→→ Wojciech Tochman, 2011,
Przekroj magazine, Art Direction:
Kasper Skirgajllo-Krajewski,
Photography: Jerzy Gumowski;
pencil, watercolour, Adobe Photoshop

*"There is no time to wait for
the inspiration when one does
editorial illustration and
the deadline is the next day."*

„Man hat keine Zeit, auf Inspirationen
zu warten, wenn man Zeitungs- und
Zeitschriftenillustrationen macht und
die Deadline am nächsten Tag abläuft.“

« Il n'y a pas de temps à perdre pour
trouver l'inspiration quand on se consacre
à l'illustration éditoriale et que la date
de livraison est le lendemain. »

←← Radiohead, 2009, *Machina* magazine,
Art Direction: Piotr Metz; pencil,
watercolour, Adobe Photoshop

→   3640 Orphans, 2008, *Przekroj*
magazine; pencil, watercolour,
Adobe Photoshop

↓   2 x 60, 2011, personal work; pencil,
watercolour, Adobe Photoshop

Michael Kutsche

1977 born in Berlin, Germany | lives and works in Berlin, Germany
http://michaelkutsche.com

*"Parallel realities, populated
by odd characters reminiscent
of movies and comics, but also
Flemish Renaissance painting."*

*„Parallelwelten, bevölkert von merkwürdigen
Figuren, die an Filme und Comics erinnern, aber
auch an Malerei der flämischen Renaissance."*

*« Réalités parallèles, peuplées d'étranges
personnages évoquant des films et des bandes
dessinées, mais aussi la peinture de
la Renaissance flamande. »*

↑ Astronauts, 2008, IDW Publishing,
book; digital painting

→ Man of Steel, 2008, personal work;
digital painting

→→ Boxer, 2008, personal work;
digital painting

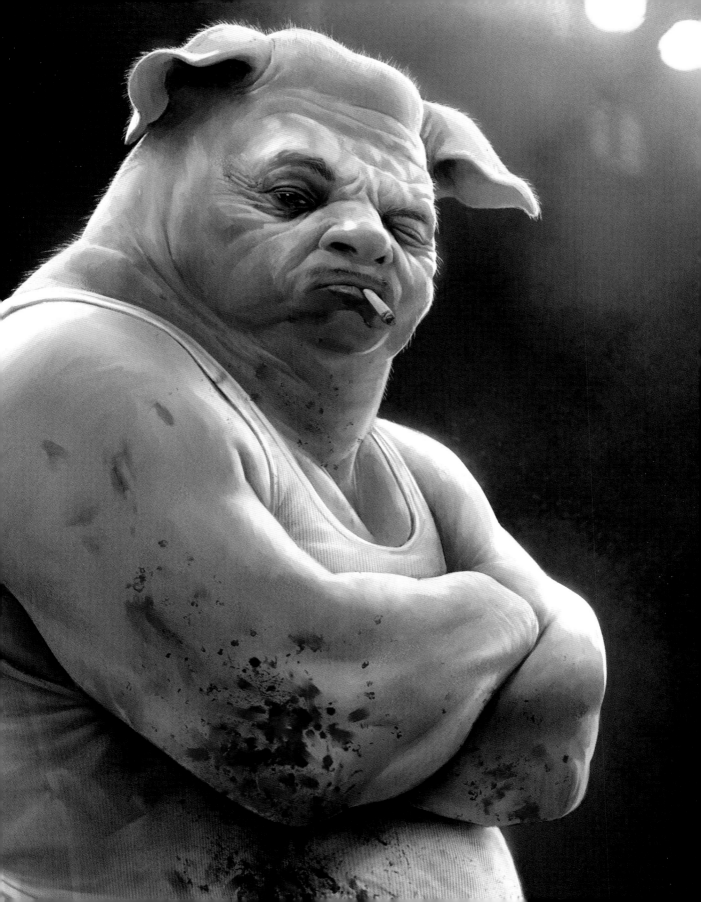

↑   Madhatter, 2008, Disney Enterprises
Inc, character design for Tim Burton's
"Alice in Wonderland"; digital painting

→   Cheshire Cat, 2008, Disney
Enterprises Inc, character design for
Tim Burton's "Alice in Wonderland";
digital painting

←← Caterpillar, 2008, Disney Enterprises
Inc, character design for Tim Burton's
"Alice in Wonderland"; digital painting

Kzeng

1988 born in Shanghai, China | lives and works in Shanghai, China
www.flickr.com/photos/kzeng119

AGENT
Zazzle
New York
www.zazzle.com

"*I like different cultures and adding certain different cultural elements into my illustrations.*"

„*Mir gefallen verschiedene Kulturen, und ich füge in meinen Illustrationen gerne bestimmte unterschiedliche kulturelle Elemente ein.*"

«*J'aime combiner des éléments culturels différents dans mes illustrations.*»

↑   Untitled, 2010, personal work;
Adobe Photoshop, Adobe Illustrator

→   Untitled, 2010, personal work;
Adobe Photoshop, Adobe Illustrator

→→ Untitled, 2010, personal work;
Adobe Photoshop, Adobe Illustrator

Laura Laakso

1979 born in Järvenpää, Finland | lives and works in Hamburg, Germany
www.lauralaakso.com

"My work is an abstraction of personal surroundings and conscious thought processes. It is a continuing experiment, using different media."

„Meine Arbeiten sind eine Abstraktion der persönlichen Umgebung und bewusster Gedankenprozesse. Ein fortdauerndes Experiment unter Verwendung verschiedener Medien."

« Mon travail est une abstraction de mon environnement personnel et de processus de réflexion conscients. C'est une expérience perpétuelle avec différentes techniques. »

↑   Untitled, 2011, personal work; mixed media, collage, pencil, acrylic

→   Untitled, 2011, personal work; mixed media, collage, pencil, acrylic

→→ Untitled, 2010, personal work; mixed media, collage, pencil, acrylic

Chrissy Lau

1984 born in Yorkshire, United Kingdom | lives and works in Sydney, Australia
www.deciphertheday.co.uk; http://deciphertheday.blogspot.com

AGENT
The Illustration Room
Sydney
www.illustrationroom.
com.au

EXHIBITIONS
1. "This Little Piggy",
China Heights, Sydney,
2010

2. "Once Upon", Ambush
Gallery, Sydney, 2009

3. Ferens Gallery, Hull,
2007

4. Beverley Art Gallery,
2006

5. Artist in residence,
Gallery 49, Bridlington,
2005–2006

*"Beautiful entrancing lines
and patterns that decorate quirky,
light-hearted subject matter."*

„Hinreißend schöne Linien und Muster
dekorieren schrullige und fröhliche Themen."

« Des lignes et des formes ravissantes
qui décorent un sujet léger et excentrique. »

↑   Gary Pepper's Shoes, 2010,
Gary Pepper Vintage; ink and pen

→   Shopper, 2011, *Pocketto*
magazine; ink and pen

→→ Ms Bird Cage, 2010,
Zest Bar; ink and pen

Jonathan Lax "Yonil"

1982 born in Holon, Israel | lives and works in Tel Aviv, Israel
www.yonil.com

↑   The Negotiation, 2010, personal
work, poster, T-shirt design; hand-drawing
and Adobe Photoshop

→   The Cycle of Indecisive Living,
2010, personal work, poster, T-shirt
design; collage, hand-drawing
and Adobe Photoshop

→→ Be on the Safe Side, 2010,
personal work, T-shirt; hand-drawing,
ink, watercolour and Adobe Photoshop

"I need my illustrations to mean something. A good-looking doodle is one thing, but I want more… I want a story behind it. I want the whole deal."

„Meine Illustrationen sollen auf jeden Fall
aussagekräftig sein. Eine gut aussehende
Kritzelei ist eine Sache, aber ich will
mehr… Ich will, dass dahinter eine
Story steht. Ich will das ganze Paket!"

« Il faut que mes illustrations aient une
signification. Faire de jolis gribouillages,
c'est bien, mais j'aspire à plus…
Il faut qu'il y ait une histoire derrière.
Je veux que ce soit complet. »

↑　Religion War, 2009, *Yedioth Ahronoth*
newspaper; hand-drawing, ink,
watercolour and Adobe Photoshop

→→　Centre of the Universe (Heart is
where the home is), 2008, personal work;
hand-drawing and Adobe Photoshop

↓　Boring wars, 2009, *Yedioth Ahronoth*
newspaper; hand-drawing, ink,
watercolour and Adobe Photoshop

Carlos Lerma

1981 born in Mazatlán, Mexico | lives and works in Tijuana and in Cancun, Mexico
www.lerms.net

EXHIBITIONS

1. "Bang!", Taller Plástica, Tijuana, 2009

2. "Paisajes de Nunca Jamás", Taller Plástica, Tijuana, 2008

3. "22", Taller Plástica, Tijuana, 2008

4. "To2onadie", Puebla, 2004

5. "Lucha de Leyendas", Tijuana, 2003

"I love telling stories. But I can't write, and I can't sing and I can't film, so I draw."

„Ich liebe es, Geschichten zu erzählen. Aber ich kann weder schreiben noch singen noch Filme drehen, also zeichne ich."

« J'adore raconter des histoires. Je ne sais pas écrire, je ne sais pas chanter et je ne sais pas faire des films, alors je dessine. »

↑ Brains Nom Nom, 2010, personal work; digital

→ Lady Justice, 2011, personal work; digital

→→ Not cold or dead, 2011, personal work; digital

↑   Los Olvidados, 2010,
personal work; digital

Mimi Leung

1982 born in Hong Kong, China | lives and works in London, United Kingdom and in Alice Springs, Australia
www.mimileung.co.uk

AGENT
Big Active
London
www.bigactive.com

EXHIBITIONS

1. "Goodbye Turdbrains", solo show, Tenderpixel Gallery, London, 2009

2. "Burst", solo show, LCX Mall, Hong Kong, 2009

3. "Hope and Struggle", solo show, Culture Club Gallery, Hong Kong, 2007

"I love energy, movement, colour and cute absurdities."

„Ich liebe Energie, Bewegung, Farbe und niedliche Absurditäten."

« J'adore l'énergie, le mouvement, la couleur et les délicieuses absurdités. »

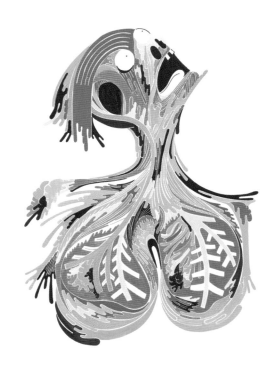

↑ Peel, 2009, *Neue* magazine; hand-drawing, gouache on paper

→ Lungs, 2011, *Mute* magazine; hand-painting, gouache on paper

→→ G2 cover, 2008, *The Guardian* newspaper; hand-drawing, gouache on paper

↑ Crowd, 2010, *Anorak* magazine; hand-drawing and digital colouring

← Guitar Crazies, 2009, Institute of Contemporary Art, London; hand-drawing, gouache on paper

→→ D.B.E., 2009, Vice; hand-drawing, gouache on paper

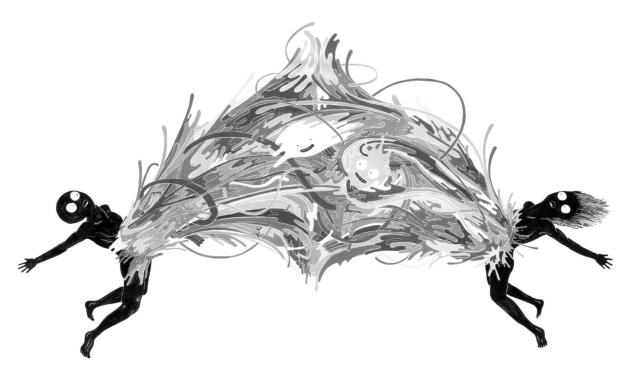

Nina Levett

1973 born in Vienna, Austria | lives and works in Vienna, Austria
www.ninalevett.com

AGENT
Artmosphere Gallery
Salzburg, Vienna
www.artmosphere.at

EXHIBITIONS

1. Artmosphere Gallery, Salzburg, 2010

2. Museum of Applied Arts, Vienna, 2010

3. Art Basel Miami, 2010

4. Art Salzburg, 2010

5. Art Monaco, 2010

"It's not about money."

„*Es geht nicht ums Geld.*"

« *Ce n'est pas une question d'argent.* »

← Wedding Ornament, 2009, personal work; Adobe Photoshop, Adobe Illustrator

→→ Self-portrait, 2011, personal work; Adobe Photoshop, Adobe Illustrator

Oscar Llorens

1975 born in Madrid, Spain | lives and works in Madrid, Spain
www.ollorens.com

AGENT 1
Colagene
Paris
www.colagene.com

AGENT 2
Capetona
Madrid
www.capetona.com

EXHIBITIONS
1. Cartográfica, Matadero, Madrid, 2011

2. Capetown, Utopic-Us, Madrid, 2010

"My work in illustration is based on the fun. I need to have it with my work."

„An Illustrationen zu arbeiten basiert auf Spaß. Den muss ich haben, wenn ich arbeite."

« Mon travail d'illustration repose sur le plaisir. Je dois en avoir quand je crée. »

↑ Wedding, 2010, personal work, wedding invitation; hand-drawing, paper, Adobe Flash, Adobe Photoshop

→ Totem 01, 2010, personal work; hand-drawing, paper, Adobe Flash, Adobe Photoshop

→→ 11-S, 2007, personal work; hand-drawing, paper, Adobe Flash, Adobe Photoshop

↑   Universe, 2010, personal work;
hand-drawing, paper, Adobe Flash,
Adobe Photoshop

→   "O" and "A", 2009, personal work;
hand-drawing, Adobe Photoshop

←←   Kaos, 2008, *Visual* magazine, cover;
hand-drawing, paper, Adobe Flash,
Adobe Photoshop

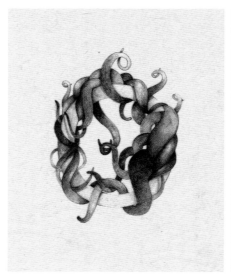

Rubens LP

1981 born in São Paulo, Brazil | lives and works in São Paulo, Brazil
www.rubenslp.com.br

AGENT
ArtBox International
Tokyo
www.artbox-int.co.jp

EXHIBITIONS
1. ArtBox, group show, Tokyo, 2010

2. ANCI, Milan, 2009

3. Absolut Brazil, 2007

4. Carnival show, London, 2007

5. 115 Gallery, Bucharest, 2007

"I'm passionate about art, colours, candies and sunny days."

„Ich habe eine Leidenschaft für Kunst, Farben, Süßigkeiten und sonnige Tage."

« Je suis passionné d'art, de couleurs, de bonbons et de journées ensoleillées. »

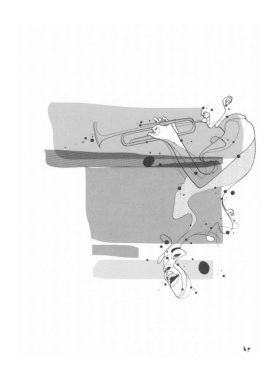

↑ Cracatua, 2008, personal work;
Adobe Illustrator

→ Jazz, 2007, personal work;
Adobe Illustrator

→→ Balance, 2005, personal work;
Adobe Illustrator

Anne Lück

1979 born in Giessen/Lahn, Germany | lives and works in Berlin, Germany
www.annelueck.com

AGENT
PLN Management
London
www.plnmanagement.com

EXHIBITIONS

1. "Punkt Punkt Komma Strich", Art Affair Gallery, Regensburg, 2010

2. "Centenary Art Collection", Alfa Romeo, 2010

3. "Deer Bln", Strychnin Gallery, Berlin, 2010

4. "Hug me, Heimlich", Filmhaus Cologne, 2009

5. "Blue", RGB Gallery, Berlin, 2008

"*I enjoy playing with elements, rearranging details and skewing proportions. A world of flying bonbons and turtles then emerges all by itself.*"

„Ich genieße es, mit Elementen zu spielen, die Details neu zu arrangieren und die Proportionen zu verdrehen. Dann erscheint ganz von allein eine Welt fliegender Bonbons und Schildkröten."

« J'aime jouer avec les éléments, réorganiser les détails et fausser les proportions. Un monde de bonbons volants et de tortues apparaît alors de lui-même. »

↑ Birdy, 2008, *Encore* magazine; Indian ink and Adobe Photoshop

→→ Candida albicans, 2008, *Jungsheft* magazine; Indian ink and Adobe Photoshop

Chris Lyons

1957 born in Buffalo (NY), USA | lives and works in New York City (NY) and in Pittsford (NY), USA
www.chrislyonsillustration.com

AGENT 1
Lindgren & Smith
New York
www.lindgrensmith.com

AGENT 2
Lemonade Illustration
London
www.lemonadeillustration.com

"A classic and sophisticated style."

„Ein klassischer und ausgefeilter Stil."

« Un style classique et sophistiqué. »

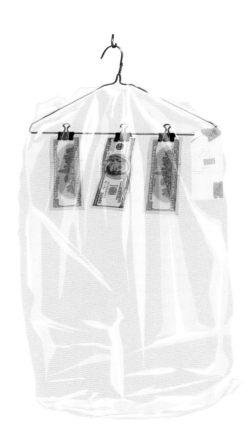

↑   Summer Music School for Kids, 2011,
Hochstein Music School; Adobe Illustrator

→   Money Laundering, 2009, *Smart Money*
magazine; Adobe Illustrator

→→ Snowy Woods, 2010, personal work;
Adobe Illustrator

Nina Maskiell

1988 born in Sydney, Australia | lives and works in Melbourne, Australia
www.ninamaskiell.com

EXHIBITIONS

1. "Spirit", solo show, Brunswick Street Gallery, Melbourne, 2011

2. "Drawn", group show, Brunswick Street Gallery, Melbourne, 2011

3. "Once Upon", group show, Ambush Gallery, Sydney, 2009

4. "All Girls", group show, Mori Gallery, Sydney, 2009

5. "Underwatery Love", group show, Gallery 285, Sydney, 2008

↑   Banksia Girl, 2009, personal work, exhibition; hand-drawing

→   Swan Girl, 2010, personal work, exhibition and website; hand-drawing

→→ Menagerie, 2010, personal work, group exhibition and website; hand-drawing

"My drawings are already there on the page just waiting for me to bring them to life. All I need to do is let the pen flow and the image grow."

„Meine Zeichnungen befinden sich bereits auf dem Blatt und warten nur noch darauf, dass ich sie zum Leben erwecke. Ich brauche nur noch den Stift laufen zu lassen, und das Bild nimmt Form an."

« Mes dessins sont déjà sur la page, ils attendent seulement que je leur donne vie. Je n'ai plus qu'à laisser le crayon suivre son cours pour que l'image prenne forme. »

Anja Mathiesen

1970 born in Hamburg, Germany | lives and works in Hamburg, Germany
www.anjamathiesen.de

"I love to combine contrasts in my pictures. What appeals to me is mixing beauty with abstract and expressive elements."

„Ich liebe es, Gegensätze in meinen Bildern zu vereinen. Die Mischung von Schönheit mit abstrakten, expressiven Elementen macht für mich den Reiz aus."

« J'adore marier des contrastes dans mes images. Le mélange de beauté et d'éléments abstraits et expressifs m'attire. »

↑ Dolce Vita, 2010, personal work; hand-drawing, marker, collage

→ Untitled, 2010, personal work; hand-drawing, watercolour, collage, marker

→→ Untitled, 2011, personal work; hand-drawing, watercolour

↑   Untitled, 2010, personal work;
hand-drawing, watercolour, crayon, marker

↖   Glam Princess, 2010, personal work;
hand-drawing, watercolour, marker, collage

→   Woman, 2010, personal work;
hand-drawing, watercolour, marker

←← Rouge, 2010, personal work;
hand-drawing, watercolour, collage

Mathiole

1986 born in Belo Horizonte, Brazil | lives and works in Belo Horizonte, Brazil
www.mathiole.com

"I like to use mixed media (traditional and digital) with strong, vivid colours and profound concepts."

„Ich setze gerne Mixed Media (traditionell und digital) mit kraftvollen, lebendigen Farben und hintergründigen Konzepten ein."

«J'aime utiliser plusieurs techniques (traditionnelles et numériques) avec des couleurs vives et des concepts profonds. »

↑   Colorphobia, 2010, personal work, poster; ink on watercolour paper

→   The Optimist, 2009, Threadless, apparel; digital illustration

→→ Alternate Ending, 2010, personal work, apparel and poster; digital

→→ Colorblind, 2008, Threadless,
apparel; mixed media

↓   For Luna, 2010, As Tall as Lions,
poster design; mixed media

↑   End, 2010, Threadless, apparel;
digital collage

→   Unlimited Imagination, 2010,
Vanguarda Clothing, apparel; digital

Maysum

1981 born in Hong Kong, China | lives and works in Hong Kong, China
www.wahahafactory.com

↑ Smoky Girl, 2009, personal work; hand-drawing, watercolour

→ Beauty2010Trendy, 2010, *Face* magazine; hand-drawing

→→ Meme Jan, 2009, exhibition; hand-drawing, watercolour

"I love colourful and funny elements so much! I would love to promote love and happiness through my creative work."

„Farbenprächtige und lustige Elemente liebe ich so sehr! Durch meine kreativen Arbeiten möchte ich Liebe und Glück fördern."

« J'aime tellement les éléments amusants et riches en couleurs ! Je voudrais que mes créations transmettent de l'amour et du bonheur. »

MC Bess

1984 born in Cannes, France | lives and works in London, United Kingdom
www.mcbess.com

AGENT
Illustrissimo
Paris
www.illustrissimo.com

EXHIBITIONS
1. "The Pirates Are Dead", Pictoplasma, Berlin, 2011

2. Gutgrinder, Rotofugi Gallery, Chicago, 2011

3. "Malevolent Melody", Concrete Hermit Gallery, London, 2010

4. "La Viande", London, 2010

5. "Meaty Melody", solo show, London, 2008

"I'm very inspired by the Fleischer Studios and the youth culture from the '80s. My illustrations usually revolve around music, sex and food."

„Mich inspirieren die Fleischer Studios und die Jugendkultur der 80er sehr. Meine Illustrationen drehen sich normalerweise um Musik, Sex und Essen."

« Je suis très inspiré par les créations de Fleischer Studios et la culture des jeunes des années 1980. Mes illustrations tournent en général autour de la musique, du sexe et de la nourriture. »

↑ Copains, 2011, Syzygy London; Adobe Photoshop

→→ Malevolent Melody Page 10, 2010, Nobrow; Adobe Photoshop

↑   20 Things That Happened
on the Internet, 2011, Syzygy London;
Adobe Photoshop

↑   Deadrusse, 2009, personal work;
Adobe Photoshop

Edward McGowan

1984 born in Glasgow, United Kingdom | lives and works in Edinburgh, United Kingdom
www.edwardmcgowan.com

AGENT
Colagene
Montreal
www.colagene.com

EXHIBITIONS
1. "Get Your Illustration Fix", L'Issue Gallery, Paris, 2011

2. Story Motel, Owl & Lion Gallery, Edinburgh 2009

3. Hidden In Plain View, Newcastle, 2008

4. Launch Party, Austin Gallery, London, 2008

5. Print Factory, Owl & Lion Gallery, Edinburgh 2008

"Sixties-style advertising meets Indian matchboxes."

„Werbung im Stil der 60er-Jahre trifft auf indische Streichholzschachteln."

« La rencontre entre la publicité des années 1960 et des boîtes d'allumettes indiennes. »

↑ Untitled, 2010, HSBC Treasury World; digital

→ Untitled, 2011, FM World; digital

→→ Role Models, 2010, *Annabelle* magazine; digital

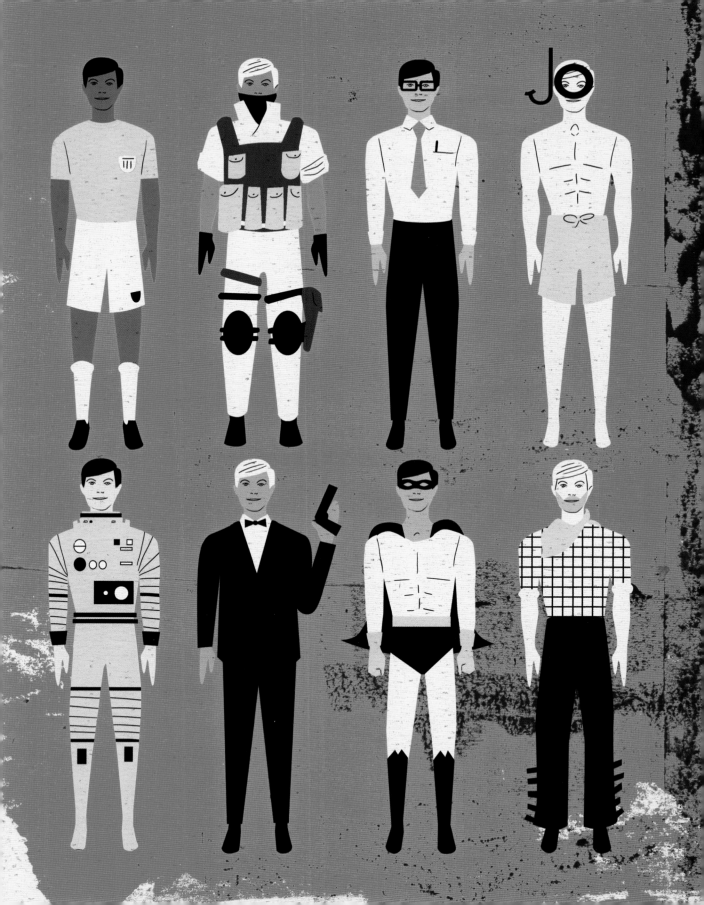

↑ Mobile Research, 2011,
Research World magazine; digital

→ → Untitled, 2010, *DBusiness*
magazine; digital

↑   Untitled, 2010, WirtschaftsWoche; digital

Jeff McMillan

1977 born in San Jose (CA), USA | lives and works in Long Beach (CA), USA
www.jeffmcmillan.com

EXHIBITIONS

1. "Suggestivism", group show, Grand Central Art Center, Santa Ana (CA), 2011

2. "Influential Element", group show, Long Beach Museum of Art, 2011

3. "Draw", group show, Museo de la Ciudad de Mexico, 2010

4. "A Maintenance of Inhabitants", solo show, Suru Gallery, Los Angeles, 2008

5. "Some Dispute over color of Hats", solo show, Fuse Gallery, New York, 2007

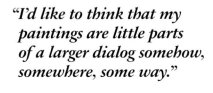

"I'd like to think that my paintings are little parts of a larger dialog somehow, somewhere, some way."

„Ich stelle mir gerne vor, dass meine Gemälde kleine Teile eines größeren Dialogs sind, der da draußen irgendwie und irgendwo stattfindet."

«J'aime penser que mes peintures sont les fragments d'un dialogue à plus grande échelle, quelque part.»

↑ Al Green, 2010, Greek Theatre, concert poster; acrylic on paper

→ Carrothead, 2011, Inle Show, Gallery 1988 curated by Greg Simkins; acrylic on paper

→→ Erykah Badu, 2010, Greek Theatre, concert poster; acrylic on paper

←← Beware Mountain, 2009,
Mountain Dew/Green Label Art,
bottle graphic series 3;
acrylic on paper

→ Secret Location, 2008,
private commission; acrylic,
oil, wood panel

↓ Passage of Mystic Rights,
2008, private commission;
acrylic, oil, wood panel

John McNally

1980 born in Liverpool, United Kingdom | lives and works in Liverpool, United Kingdom
www.johnmcnally.me

"Mundane scenes brought to life digitally to look hand-drawn. I would love a photographic memory to be able to sit and illustrate everything I see!"

„Szenen des Alltags, die digital zum Leben erweckt werden und handgezeichnet aussehen sollen. Ich hätte sehr gerne ein fotografisches Gedächtnis. Dann würde ich einfach herumsitzen und alles illustrieren, was ich sehe!"

« Des scènes banales réalisées en numérique de façon à paraître dessinées à la main. J'adorerais avoir une mémoire photographique pour m'asseoir et illustrer tout ce que je vois ! »

↑ Two Worlds AW4, 2010, Cambridge University Press, book; hand-drawing, Wacom tablet, Adobe Illustrator

→→ USP business card, 2010, USP Creative; hand-drawing, Wacom tablet, Adobe Illustrator

Javier Medellin Puyou

1977 born in San Luis Potosi, Mexico | lives and works in San Luis Potosi, Mexico
www.jilipollo.com

AGENT
Anna Goodson
Canada
www.agoodson.com

"I prefer to try and use humour, happiness and iconic references somehow in my work, never forgetting to add the eye-catching 'spark'."

„Ich versuche vor allem, Humor, Fröhlichkeit und anschauliche Abbildungen in meiner Arbeit unterzubringen und dabei als Blickfänger ein gewisses ‚Funkeln' einzubauen."

« Je préfère parier sur l'humour, le bonheur et les références emblématiques dans mon travail, sans jamais oublier d'ajouter une ‹ étincelle › accrocheuse. »

↑   Cucumber Girl, 2008, personal work;
hand-drawing and watercolour

→   Un Pitillo, 2008, personal work;
hand-drawing and watercolour

→→ Lena Juliette, 2010, personal work;
hand-drawing and ink

Nicola Meiring

1983 born in Pretoria, South Africa | lives and works in Cape Town, South Africa

AGENT
Folio Art
London
www.folioart.co.uk

EXHIBITIONS
The Bare Project,
Cape Town, 2009

↑   Serving Suggestion, 2009, Sportscene;
Adobe Illustrator

→   Ipad, 2010, *Wired* magazine;
Adobe Illustrator

→→ 2 Tier City, 2011, *Convene* magazine;
Adobe Illustrator

"Feeding from design to create iconic and graphical illustrations and imaginative typography."

„*Design wird angezapft, um sinnbildliche und grafische Illustrationen und erfinderische Typografie zu schaffen.*"

« *Je m'alimente du design pour créer des illustrations emblématiques et graphiques et une typographie imaginative.* »

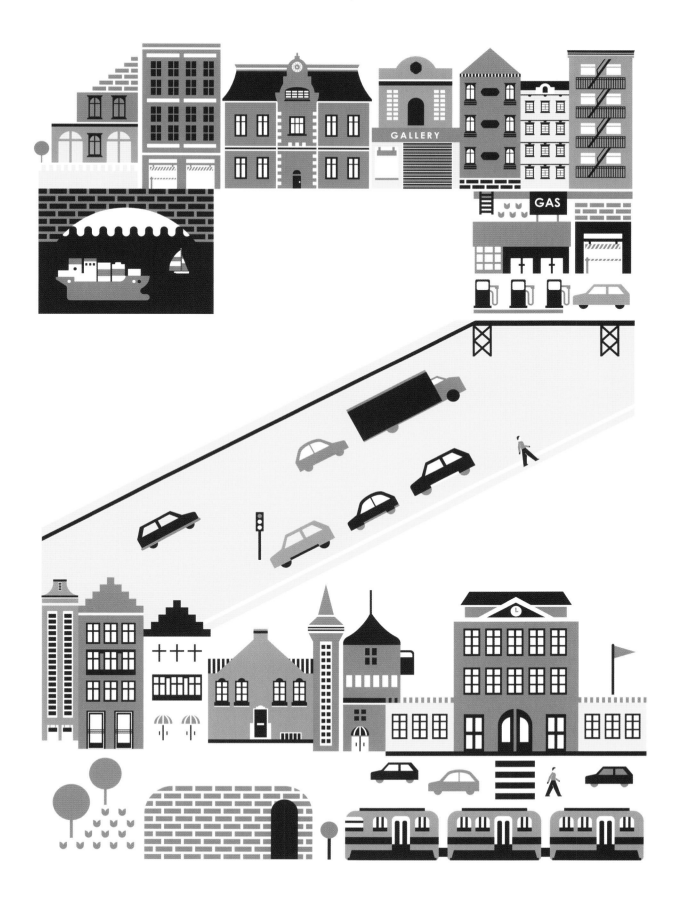

Sergio Membrillas

1982 born in Valencia, Spain | lives and works in Valencia, Spain
www.sergiomembrillas.com

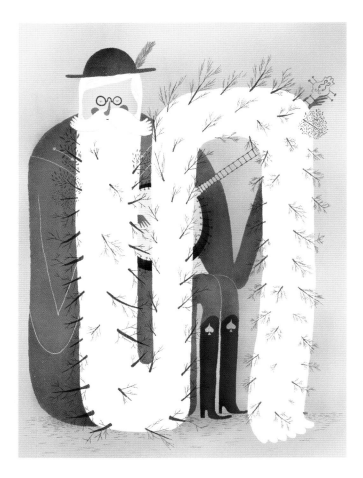

"I would define my work as a mixture of retro and naive languages combining in the pursuit of tenderness."

„Ich definiere meine Arbeit als eine Mischung aus Retro und naiven Sprachen, die sich auf der Suche nach Zärtlichkeit verbinden."

« Je peux définir mon travail comme le mélange des langages rétro et naïf qui se marient en quête de tendresse. »

↑   Old Man in the Woods, 2011, personal work; digital

→   Magic Oak (and an Owl), 2011, personal work, Beards and Trees print project; digital

→→ The Young Pianist, 2011, personal work; digital

Benjamin Mills

1986 born in Stroud, United Kingdom | lives and works in London, United Kingdom
www.benjamintmills.co.uk

EXHIBITIONS

1. Art of Nurture, Delfina, London, 2009

2. The London Show, GDi09, The Rag Factory, London, 2009

3. Graduate Degree Show, University of Brighton, 2009

"I try to evoke and record stories – both real and fictional."

„Ich versuche, Geschichten zu erwecken und festzuhalten – sowohl real als auch fiktiv.“

« Je tente d'évoquer et d'enregistrer des histoires, réelles comme fictives. »

↑ Wild Things, 2009, *Little White Lies* magazine, cover; acrylic, Adobe Photoshop

→ Aquacat, 2010, personal work; acrylic

→→ Christmas Card, 2010, personal work; acrylic

Andre Miripolsky

1951 born in Paris, France | lives and works in Los Angeles (CA), USA
www.miripolsky.com

AGENT
Smart Magna
New York
www.smartmagna.com

EXHIBITIONS
1. Monterey Historama, Museum of Monterey, Canada, 2011

2. Miripolsky+Miripolsky, DA Center for the Arts, Pomona (CA), 2008

3. Los Angeles Loteria, Aardvark Letterpress Fine Art Editions, 2008

4. Tokyo A-Go-Go!, Pop On Gallery, Tokyo, 2002

5. 25 Years Retrospective, Vincent Price Museum, Los Angeles, 2000

"It's inspiring to work with a subject I can feel a visceral connection with. In this regard I set no limits where I can go in the collaborative process. This exploration has been one of the great highlights of my creative career. Fear no art!"

„Es ist sehr inspirierend, mit einem Thema zu arbeiten, das mich tief berührt. In dieser Hinsicht grenze ich nicht ein, wohin ich im kollaborativen Prozess gehen kann. Diese Erforschung war einer der großen Höhepunkte meiner kreativen Karriere. Keine Angst vor Kunst!"

«C'est inspirant de travailler sur un sujet auquel je suis intimement lié. À cet égard, je ne marque aucune limite au cours du processus collaboratif. Cette exploration a été l'un des points culminants de ma carrière. N'ayez pas peur de l'art !»

↑   Downtown L.A. Skyline, 2005, Central City Association of Los Angeles; mixed media

→→ Angel Under Wraps, 2002, Los Angeles Public Arts Project; mixed media

Dinara Mirtalipova

1982 born in Tashkent, Uzbekistan | lives and works in Twinsburg (OH), USA
http://mirdinara.blogspot.com

EXHIBITIONS
1. American Greetings
Fine Art Show, Cleveland
(OH), 2010

"I am a big dreamer who likes to imagine unimaginable things, who draws because I can't sing and who likes telling stories through paper and pencil. I grew up on folk tales and myths and legends, there was something magical in those good old children's books my mom used to read me."

„Ich bin eine große Träumerin, die sich gerne unvorstellbare Sachen ausmalt. Ich zeichne, weil ich nicht singen kann, und ich erzähle Geschichten mit Papier und Bleistift. Ich wuchs mit Volksmärchen, Mythen und Legenden auf. Es steckte oft etwas Magisches in den guten, alten Kinderbüchern, aus denen mir meine Mutter vorlas."

« Je suis une grande rêveuse qui aime imaginer des choses inimaginables. Je dessine parce que je ne sais pas chanter et j'aime raconter des histoires avec une feuille et un crayon. J'ai grandi avec des contes, des mythes et des légendes, il y avait quelque chose de magique dans ces vieux livres pour enfants que ma mère me lisait. »

↑   Sail Away, 2010, personal work; digital

→→ Dreams, 2010, personal work; digital

↑   "Tea Time" and "Spring", 2010, personal work; digital

journey
journey
with you
with
you
with
Love

←   Journey, 2010, personal work;
pen, watercolour, digital

Elisabeth Moch

1982 born in Bonn, Germany | lives and works in Berlin, Germany
www.elisabethmoch.com

AGENT
Anja Wiroth
Berlin
www.anjawiroth.com

EXHIBITIONS
1. "Life isn't Good, It's Excellent", group show, Atelier Ahoj, Berlin, 2010

2. "Neue Probleme", group show, Galleri Kleerup, Stockholm, 2008

"I draw and travel with passion."

„Ich zeichne und reise leidenschaftlich gerne."

« Je dessine et je voyage avec passion. »

↑ Erykah Badu #1, 2010, *Uptown Strut* magazine, cover; pencil and watercolour

→→ Erykah Badu #2, 2010, *Uptown Strut* magazine, cover; pencil and watercolour

↑   Fashion Cat #1 and #2, 2010,
Chelsea magazine, fashion editorial;
pencil and Adobe Photoshop

→   Fashion Cat #3, 2010,
Chelsea magazine, fashion editorial;
pencil and Adobe Photoshop

→   Like We Were Animals,
2008, Weekday fashion store,
store interior; pencil

↓   Suzy+Carine, 2010, Vier5,
fashion show invite; pencil

Monsieur Qui

1976 born in Montreuil-sous-Bois, France | lives and works in Paris, France

AGENT
Colagene
Paris, London, Montreal
www.colagene.com

"A mix between risky ink elements and classical drawing."

„Eine Mischung aus riskanten Elementen aus Tinte und klassischer Zeichnung."

« Un mélange d'éléments osés à l'encre et de dessin classique. »

↑   Untitled, 2009, personal work; ink, pencil, Adobe Photoshop

→   Mois de Juillet, 2010, *Cosmopolitan* magazine (France); marker, Adobe Photoshop

→→ Untitled, 2009, personal work; ink, pencil, Adobe Photoshop

↑ Untitled, 2010, Dior; ink,
Adobe Photoshop

↗ Untitled, 2009, Miss Sugar
Cane; marker, Adobe Photoshop

→ Untitled, 2010, personal work;
ink, Adobe Photoshop

→→ Zoopsie, 2010, Colagene;
ink, pencil, Adobe Photoshop

Gabriel Moreno

1973 born in Baena, Spain | lives and works in Madrid, Spain
www.gabrielmoreno.com

AGENT 1
Debut Art
London, New York
www.debutart.com

AGENT 2
Bang! Bang! Studio
Moscow
www.bangbangstudio.ru

"Everything influences my work, I would say people and relations have a lot to do with it, but more important is sensuality."

„Alles beeinflusst meine Arbeit. Ich würde sagen, Menschen und Beziehungen haben viel damit zu tun, aber wichtiger noch ist Sinnlichkeit."

« Tout influence mon travail. Je dirais que les gens et les relations ont beaucoup d'impact, même si le plus important reste la sensualité. »

↑   Rafa, 2010, *Youth Vision* magazine; hand-drawing, watercolour, collage

→→ Head, 2008, personal work; hand-drawing, watercolour, paper

↘   Perfil, 2009, personal work; ink, paper

↓   Pajaro, 2009, personal work; ink, paper

← New Ibiza, 2010, Seat, advertising; hand-drawing, watercolour, Wacom tablet, Adobe Photoshop

↓ Dudamel, 2010, *Los Angeles Times* magazine; hand-drawing, Wacom tablet, Adobe Photoshop

Keiko Morimoto

1976 born in Kobe, Japan | lives and works in Lausanne, Switzerland
www.morimoto.co.uk

AGENT
Kate Larkworthy
New York
www.larkworthy.com

EXHIBITIONS

1. Galerie Pomone, group show, Lutry, 2005
2. "Keiko comes to Switzerland", Rossinière, 2004
3. Fil du temps, Rossinière, 2004
4. Mother, group show, London and Zurich, 2003

"Simple and colourful."

„Einfach und farbenprächtig."

« Simple et coloré. »

↑   Untitled, 2004, personal work; watercolour

→   Happy Days, 2004, In Good Company, website; watercolour

→→ Untitled, 2010, personal work, website; watercolour

Mar Murube

1979 born in Seville, Spain | lives and works in London, United Kingdom
www.marmurube.com

*"I look for the essence
of beauty and femininity
and interpret it in
my own terms."*

*„Ich suche nach der Essenz
von Schönheit und Weiblichkeit
und interpretiere sie auf meine
ganz persönliche Weise."*

*« Je recherche l'essence de la beauté
et de la féminité et l'interprète
dans mes propres termes. »*

↑ Welcome Spring!, 2007,
personal work, postcards; digital

→ 60s Girl, 2005, Woh; digital

→→ Eugenia Silva as the 50 ft. Woman,
2005, *ELLE* magazine; digital

Gi Myao

1979 born in London, United Kingdom | lives and works in London, United Kingdom
www.gimyao.com

AGENT
Anna Goodson
Canada
www.agoodson.com

EXHIBITIONS
"Catwalk and Backstage",
solo show, Hong Kong,
2010

"Hand-drawn illustrations are sensitive and warm. To capture an expression, an environment, the relationship between the clothing and the model is extremely powerful."

„Handgezeichnete Illustrationen sind feinfühlig und warm. Um einen Ausdruck, eine Umgebung einzufangen, ist die Beziehung zwischen Kleidung und Model extrem kraftvoll."

« Les illustrations dessinées à la main sont délicates et chaleureuses. Pour capturer une expression ou une situation, la relation entre le vêtement et le modèle est extrêmement forte. »

↑   Lady GaGa, 2010, *Milk X* magazine;
gouache on paper

→   Le Smoking, 2009, personal work;
gouache on paper

→→ Louis Vuitton Spring 2010;
gouache on paper

David Navascues

1972 born in Tolosa, Spain | lives and works in San Sebastián, Spain
www.davidnavascues.com

AGENT
Kate Larkworthy
New York
www.larkworthy.com

EXHIBITIONS
1. Creativos en Gipuzkoa, San Sebastián, 2010

2. Galería El Muro, solo show, San Sebastián, 2008

3. Galería Drum, solo show, San Sebastián, 2007

4. "What is colour", Galería Vito 021, San Sebastián, 2001

5. Certamen de artistas noveles, San Sebastián, 1999

"I like to do simple but powerful images instead of overly elaborate ones. I try to solve the illustrations in a graphic way with the emphasis on composition."

„Ich mache lieber einfache, aber kraftvolle Bilder als solche, die übermäßig ausgearbeitet sind. Ich versuche, die Illustrationen auf grafische Weise zu lösen, und betone dabei die Komposition."

«J'aime créer des images simples mais puissantes plutôt que trop élaborées. J'essaie de résoudre les illustrations de façon graphique en donnant la priorité à la composition.»

↑   Untitled, 2010, personal work; hand-drawing, digital

→   Untitled, 2010, personal work; hand-drawing, digital

→→ Untitled, 2010, personal work; hand-drawing, digital

Florian Nicolle

1986 born in Caen, France | lives and works in Caen, France
www.neo-innov.fr

> *"I try to create an image that retains its freshness from the first brush-stroke, the expressions of the line have to be very free and spontaneous."*

> *„Ich versuche, ein Bild zu schaffen, das noch die Frische des ersten Pinselstrichs in sich trägt. Der Ausdruck der Linien muss völlig frei und spontan sein."*

> *« Je tente de créer une image qui conserve la fraîcheur du premier coup de pinceau, les expressions de la ligne doivent être très libres et spontanées. »*

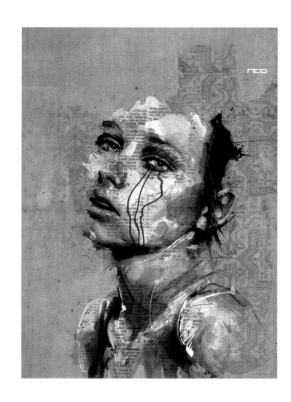

↑   Ninh Nguyen Collection, 2011, Child Education International Inc, fashion show; digital

→   Iris, 2010, personal work; digital

→→ Lil Child, 2009, personal work; digital

← Ali, 2010, personal work; digital

↓ Store, 2010, personal work; digital

→ Goldfish, 2009, Goldfish
press, book cover; digital

↘ Barack Obama, 2010,
personal work; digital

↓ Michael Jackson, 2009,
personal work; digital

FLORIAN NICOLLE **319**

Alexander Nowak

1980 born in Salzburg, Austria | lives and works in Vienna, Austria and in Hamburg, Germany
www.nowakillustration.com

AGENT
Smart Magna
Berlin
www.smartmagna.com

> *"I always try to tell a story, I draw something like a snapshot.
> I want my pictures to stimulate the fantasy and
> to give food for thought."*

*„Ich versuche immer, eine Geschichte zu erzählen. Ich zeichne so wie
ein Schnappschuss. Ich will, dass meine Bilder die Fantasie
anregen und einem was zum Nachdenken geben."*

*« J'essaie toujours de raconter une histoire, je dessine comme
s'il s'agissait d'un instantané. Je veux que mes images
stimulent la fantaisie et alimentent l'esprit. »*

↑   Indignez-Vous!, 2011, personal work;
hand-drawing, Adobe Photoshop and
Wacom tablet

→→ Oooohhh!!!, 2011, personal work;
hand-drawing, Adobe Photoshop and
Wacom tablet

Robert Palmer

1983 born in Saint-Germain-en-Laye, France | lives and works in Elancourt and in Paris, France
www.palmergd.com

AGENT
Illustrissimo
Paris
www.illustrissimo.com

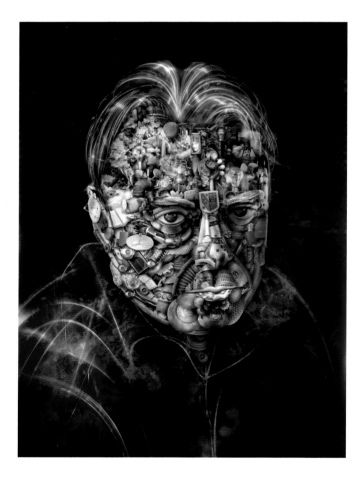

"The making of an illustration for me is like building a house or an object with Lego, with every piece having its own meaning."

„Wenn ich eine Illustration mache, ist es für mich wie das Bauen eines Hauses oder Objekts mit Lego, wobei jedes Teil seine eigene Bedeutung hat."

« Pour moi, l'élaboration d'une illustration est comme la construction d'une maison ou d'un objet en Lego, chaque élément a sa propre signification. »

↑   Christopher Hitchens, 2011, personal work; Adobe Photoshop

→   Mister Blue, 2010, Art-Cafe "Gallery" Moscow; Adobe Photoshop

→→ Never Hide, 2010, Ray-Ban; Adobe Photoshop

↑ Miss Red, 2010, Art-Cafe
"Gallery" Moscow; Adobe Photoshop

→ Pink Rubbergum, 2009,
personal work; Adobe Photoshop

←← Printemps, 2009, Printemps de
Bourges Festival; Adobe Photoshop

Sophie Parker

1988 born in Portsmouth, United Kingdom | lives and works in London, United Kingdom
www.sophie-parker.com

EXHIBITIONS

1. Latitude Festival Catwalk, Suffolk, 2010

2. Chelsea College of Art & Design Exhibition, London, 2010

3. Indigo, Paris, 2009

4. The Wallace Collection Fashion Show, London, 2009

5. Alternative Fashion Show, Spitalfields Market, London, 2008

"Playful and sensitive, my illustrations have a strong narrative element inspired by childhood memories, dreams and the cats that roam my back-garden!"

„In meinen verspielten und feinfühligen Illustrationen findet sich ein kraftvolles erzählerisches Element, inspiriert von Kindheitserinnerungen, von Träumen und den Katzen, die im Garten hinter meinem Haus herumstreunen."

« Ludiques et délicates, mes illustrations renferment un élément narratif puissant, inspiré de mes souvenirs d'enfance, de mes rêves et des chats qui rôdent dans le jardin ! »

↑ Sweet Dreams, 2011, personal work; hand-drawing, pencil, pen, markers, Adobe Photoshop

→ Helping Hand, 2011, personal work; hand-drawing, pencil, pen, markers, Adobe Photoshop

→→ Little Vixen, 2011, personal work; hand-drawing, pencil, pen, markers, Adobe Photoshop

Laura Pérez

1984 born in Valencia, Spain | lives and works in Valencia, Spain
www.lauraperez.es

AGENT 1
Anna Goodson
Canada
www.agoodson.com

AGENT 2
Pencil Ilustradores
Spain
www.pencil-ilustradores.com

EXHIBITIONS
1. "Art Sport", group show, Calgary

2. Journée des portes Ouvertes, École Régionale des Beaux Arts, Rennes

3. "I el futur que ens espera", Barcelona

4. Market Collective, Calgary

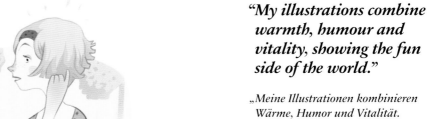

"My illustrations combine warmth, humour and vitality, showing the fun side of the world."

„Meine Illustrationen kombinieren Wärme, Humor und Vitalität. Sie zeigen die lustige Seite der Welt."

« Mes illustrations combinent chaleur, humour et vitalité pour montrer la face amusante du monde. »

↑ Walking, 2010, personal work; Adobe Photoshop

→ At the exhibition, 2010, personal work; Adobe Photoshop

→→ Coffee, 2010, *Coup de Pouce* magazine; Adobe Photoshop

Lorenzo Petrantoni

1971 born in Milan, Italy | lives and works in Milan, Italy
www.lorenzopetrantoni.com

EXHIBITIONS
Moooi Gallery,
Amsterdam, 2010

"*I love old books. I want to bring them back to life, discover their stories and tell the present through the past.*"

„*Ich liebe alte Bücher. Ich will sie wieder zum Leben erwecken, ihre Geschichten erkunden und die Gegenwart durch die Vergangenheit erzählen lassen.*"

«*J'aime les vieux livres. Je veux leur offrir une seconde vie, découvrir leurs histoires et raconter le présent à travers le passé.*»

↑ Ragtime Musical, Broadway, 2010; collage

→ *Newsweek* magazine, 2009, cover; collage

→→ *Circle* magazine, 2010; collage

Marta Pieczonko

1980 born in Warsaw, Poland | lives and works in Cologne, Germany and in Warsaw, Poland
www.martapieczonko.com

EXHIBITIONS

1. Passagen, Studio Wow, Cologne, 2011

2. "Inside out", Gallery Milano, Warsaw, 2010

3. "Auf dem laufenden Band", Galerie im Turm, Cologne, 2010

4. "30 x 30", Gallery Milano, Warsaw, 2010

5. "Coincidence II", Ignis, European Cultural Center, Cologne, 2009

"I am looking for ways of expression that make my illustrations more sensual. And I like it when the humorous and mysterious come together."

„Ich suche nach Ausdrucksmöglichkeiten, die meine Illustrationen sinnlicher machen. Und mir gefällt es, wenn das Humorvolle und das Mysteriöse aufeinandertreffen."

« Je cherche des modes d'expression qui rendent mes illustrations plus sensuelles. Et j'aime quand l'humour se marie au mystère. »

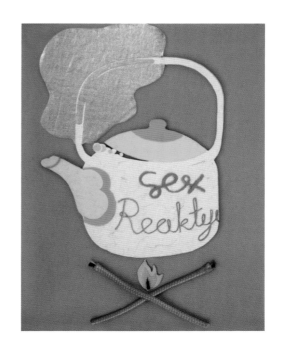

↑ Kite, 2011, *Polityka* magazine; fabric collage

→ Sex Reakty, 2011, *Zwierciadlo* magazine; fabric collage

→→ Superwoman, 2011, *Zwierciadlo* magazine; fabric collage

Domenico Principato

1987 born in Syracuse, Italy | lives and works in Milan, Italy
www.wix.com/domenicoprincipato/portfolio

EXHIBITIONS

1. White Milano Show,
Fashion Trade Show, 2010

2. Ethical Fashion Show,
Carrousel du Louvre,
Paris, 2008

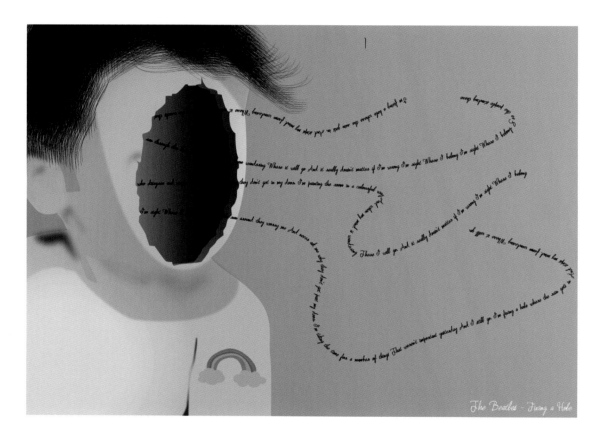

*"My illustrations try to represent certain aspects
of our society through both a communicative
and a conceptual use of images."*

*„Meine Illustrationen versuchen, bestimmte Aspekte unserer
Gesellschaft zu repräsentieren, indem Bilder sowohl
kommunikativ als auch konzeptionell verwendet werden."*

*« Mes illustrations tentent de représenter certains aspects
de notre société grâce à une utilisation communicative
et conceptuelle des images. »*

↑ Fixing a Hole, 2010, IED;
hand-drawing, Adobe Illustrator

→→ Untitled, 2010, personal work;
hand-drawing, photo, paper,
Adobe Photoshop

334

Adam Quest

1982 born in Poznan, Poland | lives and works in Poznan, Poland
www.adamquest.eu

AGENT
Lemonade Illustration
London
www.lemonadeillustration.com

"I make vintage old-looking pictures and designs. I love the simplicity of shapes and colour mixed with scratches, dust, and paper texture."

„Meine Bilder und Designs wirken retro und sind auf Alt getrimmt. Ich liebe die Einfachheit von Formen und Farben und mische Kratzer, Staub und die Beschaffenheit des Papiers hinein."

«Je crée des images et des designs vintage. J'aime la simplicité des formes et des couleurs assorties d'éraflures, de poussière et de textures de papier.»

↑ Facegod, 2010, AX Shop, T-shirt; mixed media, Adobe Photoshop, Adobe Illustrator

→ Summertime, 2010, personal work; mixed media, Adobe Photoshop, Adobe Illustrator

→→ Open your mind, 2010, personal work; mixed media, Adobe Photoshop, Adobe Illustrator

Jason Raish

1981 born in Seoul, South Korea | lives and works in New York (NY), USA and in Tokyo, Japan
www.jasonraish.com

"My artwork is the result of trying to break the bonds of years of photorealistic art-school teaching, although some of it still remains."

„Meine Kunst ist der Versuch, die Ketten des jahrelangen fotorealistischen Unterrichts der Kunsthochschule zu sprengen, obwohl noch so manches davon hängen bleibt."

« Mon œuvre naît de la rupture avec des années d'enseignement du photoréalisme, même s'il en reste quelques traces. »

↑   Paris Fade-Away Girl, 2009,
Saatchi and Saatchi New York;
pencil, paper and acrylic

→   Ella, 2008, Hartford Courant;
pencil, paper and acrylic

→→ Yahoo! Elephants, 2008, Yahoo!
Singapore; pencil, paper, acrylic,
ink and Adobe Photoshop

338

←← Shanghai Wishtree Girl, 2008,
personal work; pencil, paper and acrylic

→ Yahoo! Bamboo Birdman, 2009,
Yahoo! Singapore; pencil, paper, acrylic,
ink and Adobe Photoshop

↓ Tiger Beer Culture, 2008,
Tiger Beer; pencil, paper, acrylic,
ink and Adobe Photoshop

Eduardo Recife

1980 born in Belo Horizonte (MG), Brazil | lives and works in Belo Horizonte (MG), Brazil
www.eduardorecife.com; www.misprintedtype.com

EXHIBITIONS

1. "Do Outro Lado", group show, Brazilian Embassy, Tokyo, 2010

2. Retroism, group show, Retrospect Gallery, Gold Coast, 2010

3. Brazilian Illustration, group show, Gallery 23, London, 2009

4. Art Trek 3, solo show, Galerie Mekanik, Antwerp, 2007

5. Junta Show, group show, Scion Gallery, Culver City, 2006

↑   You Are Not Alone, 2009, personal work; digital collage

→   My Love for You, 2010, personal work; digital collage

→→ I Want You, 2009, personal work; digital collage

"I believe drawing is what I do best. It's also the best way for me to communicate things I can't find words for… It's a sort of therapy, a hobby, a job, it's what makes me happy."

„Ich glaube, Zeichnen kann ich am besten. Es ist für mich auch der beste Weg, um all das zu kommunizieren, für das ich keine Worte finde… eine Art Therapie, ein Hobby, ein Job… und es macht mich einfach glücklich."

«Je crois que dessiner est ce que je fais de mieux. C'est aussi la meilleure façon de communiquer des choses pour lesquelles je ne trouve pas les mots. C'est une sorte de thérapie, un hobby, un travail, c'est ce qui me rend heureux.»

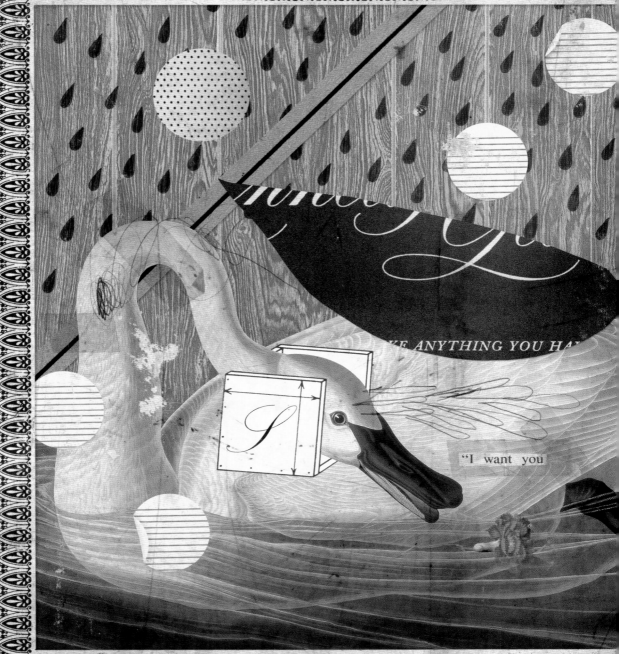

KE ANYTHING YOU HA

"I want you

Lying

Adriano Renzi

1973 born in Rio de Janeiro (RJ), Brazil | lives and works in Rio de Janeiro (RJ), Brazil
www.adrianorenzi.com

EXHIBITIONS

1. IlustraBrasil #6 and #7,
São Paulo/Rio de Janeiro,
2011

2. Bonequinhos Viajantes,
Rio de Janeiro, 2011

3. O Mundo Encantado
de Adriano Renzi,
Teresópolis, 2010

4. Sueños en Papel,
Jalisco, 2008

*"I try to put on paper all my childhood memories
and imagination. I have never stopped
daydreaming and my watercolours
are the way I have found to express it."*

*„Ich versuche, all meine Kindheitserinnerungen und Fantasie
auf Papier zu bringen. Ich habe nie aufgehört, mit offenen
Augen zu träumen, und ich kann das am besten
mit meinen Wasserfarben ausdrücken."*

*« J'essaie de mettre sur le papier tous mes souvenirs d'enfance
et mon imagination. Je suis un éternel rêveur et j'ai trouvé
dans mes aquarelles le moyen de m'exprimer. »*

↑ Death of Bumba Meu Boi, 2006,
Rocco Publishing (Rio de Janeiro),
children's book; watercolour and
watercolour pencil on paper

→→ Freedom to the Golden Bird,
2008, São José dos Campos city's
education programme; watercolour
and watercolour pencil on paper

Janine Rewell

1986 born in Helsinki, Finland | lives and works in Helsinki, Finland
www.janinerewell.com

AGENT
Agent Pekka
Helsinki
www.agentpekka.fi

EXHIBITIONS

1. Finnish Design Awards 2011, Grafia & Ornamo, Helsinki

2. Open 140, University of Art and Design, Helsinki, 2011

3. Beyond Gravity, Vallery Gallery, Barcelona, 2010

4. 20 under 30, *Print* magazine, New York, 2010

5. Best of the Year, Grafia, Helsinki, 2009

> *"Geometric vector forms, bright colours and details, often filled with enchanting textures."*

> *„Geometrische Vektorformen, leuchtende Farben und Details, oft gefüllt mit zauberhaften Texturen.“*

> *« Formes vectorielles géométriques, couleurs vives et détails, souvent complétés de textures ravissantes. »*

↑   Letter S, 2011, Kärkimedia, advertising; Adobe Photoshop and Adobe Illustrator

→   Season' Greetings, 2011, Mattmo Concept & Design; Adobe Photoshop and Adobe Illustrator

→→ Untitled, 2011, *Brummel* mgazine, cover; Adobe Photoshop and Adobe Illustrator

El Niño Rodríguez

1969 born in Rosario, Argentina | lives and works in Buenos Aires, Argentina
www.elninorodriguez.com

EXHIBITIONS

1. "200 Años Rediseñados", Casa de las Américas, Madrid, 2010

2. "Una Patria de Diez Plazas", Palais de Glace, Buenos Aires, 2010

3. Argentinian Comics, Argentine pavilion, Frankfurt Book Fair, 2010

4. One Dot Zero, Buenos Aires, 2007

5. Pictoplasma, Berlin, 2006

"I love pop. Anything goes in pop: political ideas, comics, advertising and even porn share this world of strong and instantly recognisable images."

„Ich liebe Pop. In Pop geht alles: Politische Ideen, Comics, Reklame und sogar Porno teilen sich diese Welt der starken und sofort erkennbaren Bilder."

« J'aime le style pop, qui va avec tout : opinions politiques, bandes dessinées, publicité, voire porno, tous partagent ce monde d'images fortes et immédiatement reconnaissables. »

↑ Dead Massera, 2010, Antifichus, Editorial Pequeño Editor, book; hand-drawing and Adobe Illustrator

→ Magenta Overflow, 2008, personal work; hand-drawing and Adobe Illustrator

→→ Betty, 2008, *Fierro* magazine, cover; hand-drawing and Adobe Illustrator

Emmanuel Romeuf

1982 born in Saint-Denis de la Réunion, France | lives and works in Paris, France
www.emmanuelromeuf.fr

AGENT
Illustrissimo
Paris
www.illustrissimo.fr

EXHIBITIONS
1. "20 under 30", *Print* magazine, New York, 2010

2. Sismic festival, Sierre, 2009

3. BD Fils, Lausanne, 2008

4. Festival International de la Bande Dessinée, Angoulême, 2006–2008

5. Ilustrarte, Barreiro, 2005

"Versatility. Most of the time digital with gradients and pastel colours."

„Vielseitigkeit. Meistens digital mit Farbverläufen und Pastellfarben."

« Versatilité. Le plus souvent numérique, avec des dégradés et des couleurs pastel. »

↑ Fêtes de Bayonne, 2007, poster; digital

→→ The Gold Rush, 2009, personal work; digital

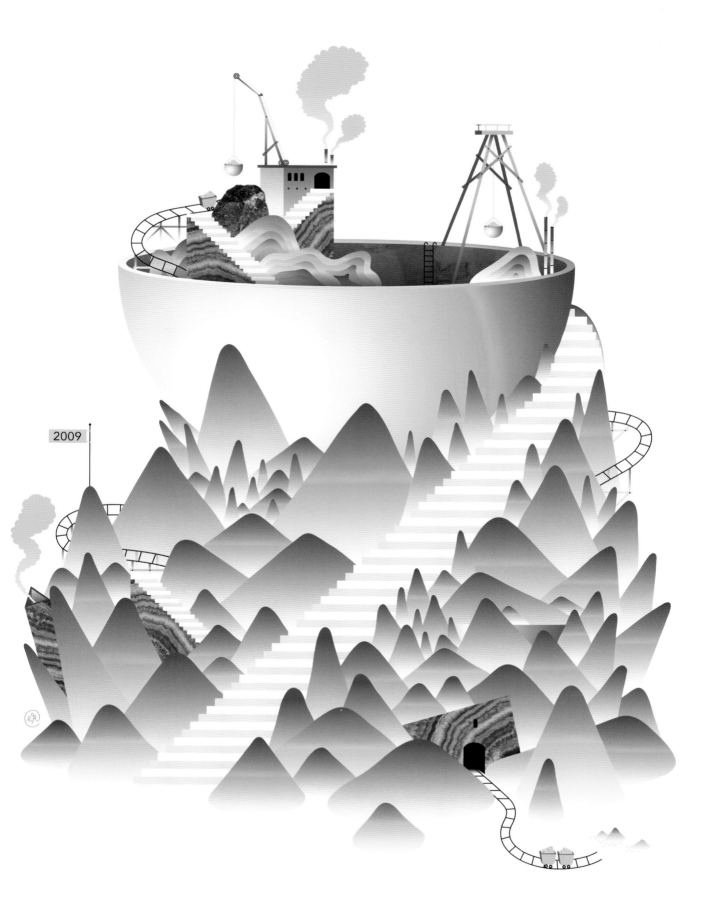

2009

Paul Ryding

1981 born in Glasgow, United Kingdom | lives and works in Glasgow, United Kingdom
www.paulryding.com

"I don't use sketchbooks. I rarely plan ahead. I get a loose idea of what I want and run with it. That said, it is more of a slow shuffle than a run."

„Ich verwende keine Skizzenbücher. Nur selten plane ich voraus. Ich kriege eine ungefähre Idee davon, was ich will, und lasse mich dann einfach davon treiben. Der Prozess ist also eher ein langsames Schlurfen als ein Laufen."

« Je n'utilise pas de carnets à croquis. J'anticipe rarement. J'ai une idée vague de ce que je veux et je pars de là. Ceci dit, le parcours est une marche lente plutôt qu'une course. »

↑ Y'all Is Fantasy Island, personal work, 2007; graphite and gouache

→→ Smash the State, 2011, *The Idler* magazine; pencil and gouache

←   Ulla, 2009, personal work; graphite

↓   Kat, 2007, The Arches Gallery; graphite and gouache

↑ DJ Esa, 2007, *The Skinny* magazine;
graphite and gouache

→ Elaine, 2007, personal work;
graphite and gouache

Susanne Saenger

1967 born in Karlsruhe, Germany | lives and works in Karlsruhe, Germany
www.susanne-saenger.de

AGENT
Kate Larkworthy
New York
www.larkworthy.com

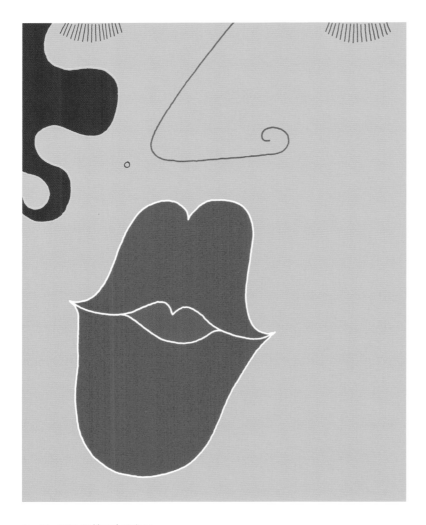

"Illustrative and graphic problem-solving with bright colours and clear lines. And humour if possible."

„Illustrative und grafische Problemlösung mit leuchtenden Farben und klaren Linien. Und Humor, wenn möglich."

« Résoudre les problèmes graphiques et d'illustration avec des couleurs vives et des lignes nettes. Et de l'humour, dans la mesure du possible. »

↑   Kiss, 2004, *Süddeutsche Zeitung*
magazine; mixed media

→   Untitled, 2001, Philips, book;
mixed media

→→ Untitled, 2000, *Geo Wissen*
magazine; mixed media

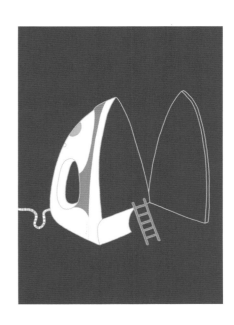

Kouzou Sakai

1977 born in Hyuga, Japan | lives and works in Yokohama, Japan
www.kouzou.org

*"My illustration is based on peace
and is coloured with elements
such as beauty, nostalgia, delight."*

*„Meine Illustrationen beruhen auf Frieden
und sind koloriert mit solchen Elementen
wie Schönheit, Nostalgie und Wonne."*

*« Mes illustrations évoquent la paix
et sont enrichies de concepts comme
la beauté, la nostalgie et le plaisir. »*

↑   Ice Club, 2009, GignoSystem Japan,
Inc; Adobe Illustrator

→   Susukigahara, 2008, GignoSystem
Japan, Inc; Adobe Illustrator

→→ Sun, 2009, Portal Co. Ltd;
Adobe Illustrator

Graham Samuels

1975 born in Southend, United Kingdom | lives and works in Stockholm, Sweden
www.grahamsamuels.com

AGENT 1
Art Department
New York
www.art-dept.com

AGENT 2
Serlin Associates
London
www.serlinassociates.com

AGENT 3
Agent Bauer
Stockholm
www.agentbauer.com

"My illustrations are bold and colourful, yet detailed and nuanced, and always hand-drawn. I am inspired by vintage paperbacks, LPs and film posters."

„Meine Illustrationen sind gewagt und farbenprächtig und doch detailliert und nuanciert, aber immer handgezeichnet. Mich inspirieren alte Taschenbücher, LPs und Filmplakate."

« Mes illustrations sont audacieuses et riches en couleurs, mais aussi détaillées et nuancées et toujours dessinées à la main. Je m'inspire des vieux livres de poche, des disques vinyle et des affiches de films. »

↑   Affairs of Business, 2010, *The Telegraph* magazine; pencil and acrylic on paper

→   Cry Bear, 2010, Naturskyddsföreningen, advertisement; pencil and acrylic on board

→→ Dream of a Gentlemen's Island, 2009, Dramaten, poster; acrylic on board

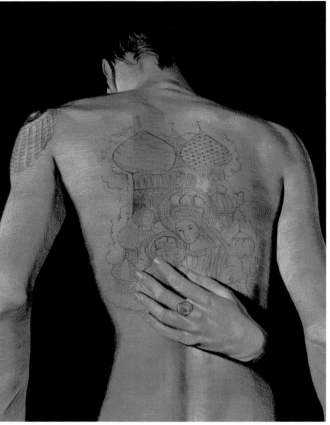

↑   Romanov Must Die, 2008, *Fashion Tale*
magazine, Stylist: Carl-Axel Wahlstrom,
Models: Leon L./Mikas, Ronnia F./Elite;
pencil and acrylic on paper

↑   The Sandcastle, 2010,
personal work; acrylic on board

David Sandlin

1956 born in Belfast, United Kingdom | lives and works in New York (NY), USA
www.davidsandlin.com

"I'm a printmaker with a populist bent – comics and illustration are a natural outgrowth of that."

„Ich bin Grafiker mit einer populistischen Neigung… Comics und Illustrationen sind davon die natürlichen Früchte."

«Je suis un graveur avec un penchant populiste, et mes bandes dessinées et illustrations en découlent naturellement.»

↑ Subway Ghost, 2010, School of Visual Arts, poster, Art Direction: Michael Walsh; ink and digital

→ Heavenly Ride, 2010, School of Visual Arts, poster, Art Direction: Michael Walsh; ink and digital

→→ House of Debt, 2011, *Strapazin* magazine; ink and digital

↑   Stimul-U.S., 2009, *The New York Times* newspaper, Art Direction: Leeann Shapton; ink and digital

↖   Stimulus Package Store, 2009, *The New York Times* newspaper, Art Direction: Leeann Shapton; ink and digital

↑   Belfast Belle Past, 2008,
personal work; oil on canvas

↓   He Coveted My Wife, 2006,
Fantagraphics, book: "An Alphabetical
Ballad of Carnality" by David Sandlin;
ink and digital

Nicholas Saunders

1984 born in Manchester, United Kingdom | lives and works in London, United Kingdom
www.nicholassaunders.co.uk

AGENT
Folio Art
London
www.folioart.co.uk

EXHIBITIONS
1. Toy Made One,
Berlin, 2010

2. UK Young Artists,
Skopje, 2009

3. Fedrigoni, London, 2008

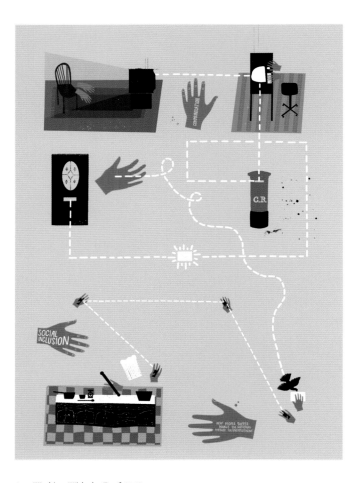

↑ Working With the Deaf, 2010,
Big Issue magazine; digital

→ Contact, 2009, Green House,
website; digital

→→ S.F.O. , 2011, *Campden FO*
magazine, Campden Media; digital

*"Traditional screen-printing
and digital."*

„Traditioneller Siebdruck
und Digitales."

« Sérigraphie traditionnelle
et numérique. »

↑ Moving Jobs, 2011, *CPO Agenda*
magazine, Redactive Media; digital

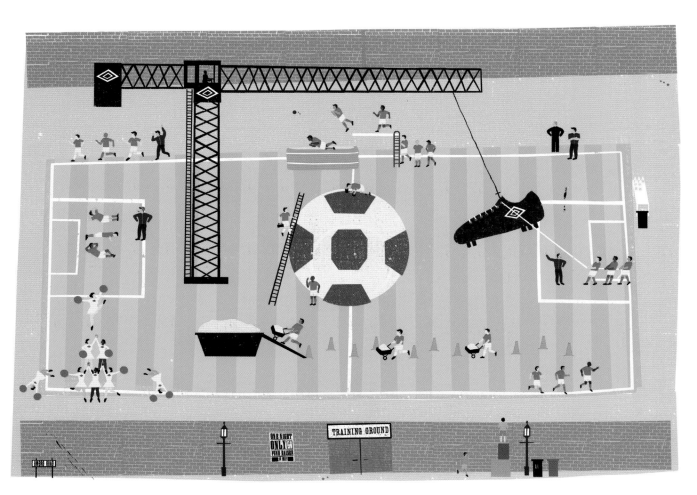

↑   Training Ground Culture, 2010,
Umbro, advertising; digital

Frederick Sebastian

1964 born in Ottawa (ON), Canada | lives and works in Ottawa (ON), Canada
http://fredericksebastian.blogspot.com

EXHIBITIONS

1. International Editorial Cartoon Competition Press Freedom, Ottawa, 2011

2. Nocturne, Cube Gallery, Ottawa, 2009

3. World Press Cartoon, Sintra, 2009

4. World Press Cartoon, Sintra, 2008

5. Iconoclast, Cube Gallery, Ottawa, 2006

"It's a never-ending quest to marry spontaneity with precision. When it works it's magic."

„Es ist eine nie endende Suche danach, Spontaneität mit Präzision zu vermählen. Funktioniert es, ist es wie ein Zauber."

« Il s'agit d'une quête sans fin pour allier spontanéité et précision. Quand cela fonctionne, c'est magique. »

↑ Tom Cruise, 2007, personal work; graphite stick on paper

→ Gaddafi, 2011, *The Toronto Star* newspaper; charcoal on mylar, eraser

→→ File By EX: Meeting organizer, 2010, *The Ottawa Citizen* newspaper; Chinese ink sticks, oil pastel, dip pens, commercial ink

↑   The Good Lawyer, 2010, *Ottawa*
magazine, Art Direction: Jane Corbett;
acrylic on canvas

→   Burmese Veterans, 2009, *Legion*
magazine, Art Direction: Jason Duprau;
palette knife, brushes, acrylic

←← Doing When There Is Nothing
To Be Done, 2011, *Canadian Medical
Association Journal* newspaper; palette
knife, brushes, acrylics

Marie-Adelyne Seillier

1984 born in Ciney, Belgium | lives and works in Brussels, Belgium

"I'm rarely satisfied when I draw. That's why I enjoy spending hours cutting and pasting old pattern paper, vintage magazines and scientific books."

„Ich bin selten zufrieden, wenn ich zeichne. Darum genieße ich es auch, stundenlang alte Musterpapiere, Magazine und wissenschaftliche Bücher auszuschneiden und neu zusammenzukleben."

« Je suis rarement satisfait quand je dessine. C'est pourquoi j'adore passer des heures à découper et coller de vieux papiers peints, des magazines vintage et des livres scientifiques. »

↑ The End, 2009, personal work; collage and gesso

→→ White Paw, 2009, personal work; collage

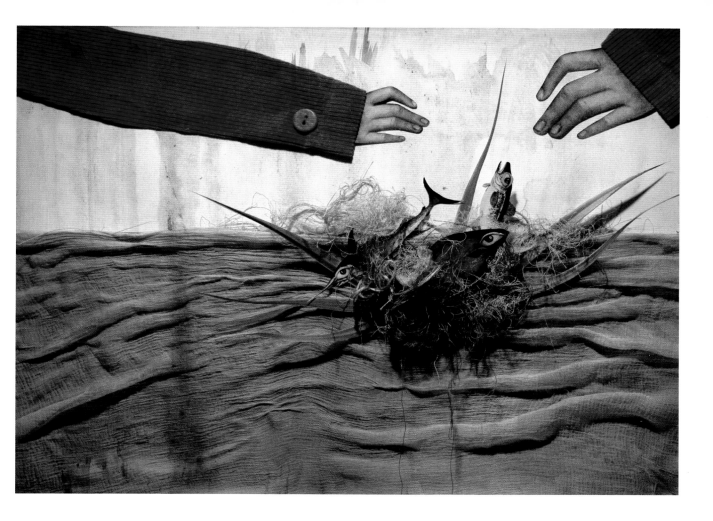

↑   Rescue, 2010, personal work;
collage, paper, fabric, thread

→   Wanted, 2010, personal work; collage

←← For Everyone a Single Tear, 2010,
Pop Corn Mag&Zine, "Death" issue, magazine
article; Adobe Photoshop, scanner, old books

Alberto Seveso

1976 born in Milan, Italy | lives and works in Milan, Italy
www.burdu976.com

"I don't have any idea about my work. I don't know how to describe my work. Everyone is free to understand or misunderstand my illustrations."

„Von meiner Arbeit habe ich keine Ahnung. Ich wüsste nicht, wie ich sie beschreiben sollte. Jeder kann meine Illustrationen nach Belieben begreifen oder auch missverstehen.“

« Je ne sais rien de mon travail. Je ne sais pas comment le décrire. Tout le monde est libre de comprendre ou non mes illustrations. »

↑   Coppia di Bagasce, 2007,
personal work; Adobe Illustrator
and Adobe Photoshop

→   Kelly Slater, 2008, *Relentless* magazine;
Adobe Illustrator and Adobe Photoshop

→→ David Lynch, 2009, Factory311
Evolution exhibition; Adobe Illustrator
and Adobe Photoshop

Ashkahn Shahparnia

1984 born in Los Angeles (CA), USA | lives and works in Los Angeles (CA), USA
www.ashkahn.com

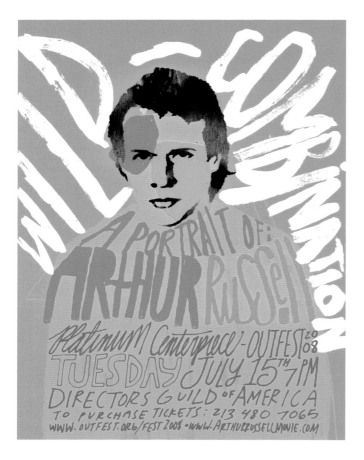

↑   Arthur Russell, 2009,
Wild Combination / Matt Wolf,
movie poster; brush and digital

→   I Don't Understand, 2011,
personal work, greeting card;
brush, paper and digital

→→ Kitten, 2011, Kitten Music,
poster; marker, paper and digital

"Simplify, simplify, simplify…
to arrive at the essence of the idea."

„*Vereinfachen, vereinfachen, vereinfachen…*
um zur Quintessenz der Idee zu gelangen."

« *Simplifier, simplifier, simplifier…*
pour parvenir à l'essence de l'idée. »

Daniel Sims

1987 born in Kettering, United Kingdom | lives and works in London, United Kingdom
www.dan-sims.co.uk

EXHIBITIONS
1. Chelsea College of
Art & Design Exhibition,
London, 2010

"Directly inspired by my experiences as a music photographer, I aim to capture the unique energy and emotion of live music."

„Mich inspirieren unmittelbar meine Erfahrungen als Musikfotograf, und ich will die einzigartige Energie und Emotion von Livemusik einfangen."

« Directement inspiré de mes expériences comme photographe de musiciens, j'aime capter l'énergie et l'émotion uniques d'un concert en direct. »

↑ Biffy Clyro, 2010, personal work;
hand-drawing, ink, pen, pencil and
Adobe Photoshop

→ Lola, 2010, personal work;
hand-drawing, ink, pen, pencil
and Adobe Photoshop

→→ M.I.A. 2, 2011, personal work;
hand-drawing, ink and Adobe Photoshop

Kelly Smith

1985 born in Hobart, Australia | lives and works in Hobart, Australia
www.birdyandme.com.au

AGENT
Illustration Ltd
London
www.illustrationweb.com

EXHIBITIONS

1. "Drawn From Fashion", group show, Finders Keepers, Melbourne, 2011

2. "Curvy 7", group show, Magnation, Sydney, 2010

3. "Disband", group show, amBUSH Gallery, Sydney, 2010

4. "A Tale of Two Kellys", Per Square Metre, Collingwood, 2009

5. "Where the Wild Things Are", solo show, 696 Gallery, Melbourne, 2008

"My work sits somewhere between the imperfection of art and the detailed realism of a photograph. It's about capturing beauty in a graphic form."

„Meine Arbeiten stehen irgendwo zwischen der Unvollkommenheit von Kunst und dem detaillierten Realismus eines Fotos. Es geht darum, Schönheit in ihrer grafischen Form festzuhalten."

« Mon travail oscille entre l'imperfection de l'art et le réalisme détaillé de la photographie. Il cherche à capturer la beauté sous une forme graphique. »

↑ Come Fly With Me, 2010, personal work; hand-drawing, pencil, pastel and Adobe Photoshop

→ On the Prowl, 2010, personal work; hand-drawing, pencil and watercolour

→→ Sadako, 2011, personal work; hand-drawing, pencil, watercolour and Adobe Photoshop

Spig

1972 born in Marseille, France | lives and works in Paris, France

AGENT
Agent 002
Paris
www.agent002.com

*"When I paint, I like the sheer size of the environment,
always very spectacular with a great sense of scale."*

„*Wenn ich male, gefällt mir einfach schon, wie groß die Umgebung ist,
immer sehr spektakulär mit einem tollen Sinn für Proportionen.*"

«*Quand je peins, j'aime l'ampleur de l'environnement, toujours
très spectaculaire, avec un grand sens de l'échelle.*»

↑ 51N4E, 2010; 3D
and Adobe Photoshop

→→ Arigon, 2009, EM2N;
3D and Adobe Photoshop

Iker Spozio

1972 born in Luino, Italy | lives and works in San Sebastián, Spain
www.ikerspozio.net

AGENT
Folio Art
London
www.folioart.co.uk

EXHIBITIONS
1. "10 Years of Work",
Garabat Gallery, Bilbao,
2011

2. "The Rose-Eaters",
Shibuya Gallery, Tokyo,
2010

3. "Paga Extra", at Flow
Space, San Sebastián, 2010

4. "Walls of Sound", Drum
Gallery, San Sebastián, 2006

5. "Desafinado", Drum
Gallery, San Sebastián, 2004

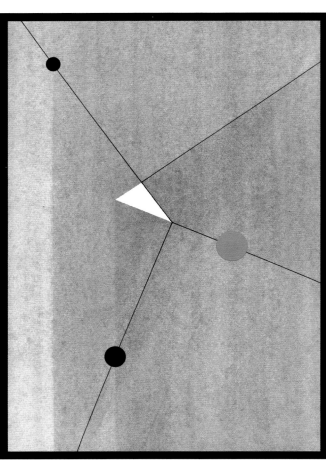

*"Extremely diverse and informed
illustration, engraved and painted
with a vast spectrum of influences
and inspirations."*

*„Extrem unterschiedliche und sachkundige
Illustrationen, aus einem riesigen Spektrum
von Einflüssen und Inspirationen gespeist
und dann eingraviert und gemalt."*

*« Des illustrations extrêmement variées
et riches, gravées et peintes selon un large
spectre d'influences et d'inspirations. »*

↑ Abstract Composition, 2011,
personal work; Indian ink

→ When You're Here You're Family,
2009, Dirty Projectors, poster; engraving

→→ Village, 2011, *The Tip of the Knife*
magazine; collage and monotype

Olivier Tafforin

1975 born in Toulouse, France | lives and works in London, United Kingdom
www.oliviertafforin.com

EXHIBITIONS

1. Richard Laurence
Interiors, Spitalfields,
London, 2008

2. The Chelsea Art Gallery,
London, 2007

3. On the Wall Art Fair,
London Olympia
Exhibition Centre, 2004

4. DB international Fine
Art Gallery, London, 2003

*"Through paint I make my
mind's little cinematographic
stories visually accessible. My
love for vintage glamour is very
often reflected in my work."*

*„Durch Malerei mache ich die kleinen,
filmischen Geschichten aus meinem Kopf
visuell zugänglich. Meine Liebe für
altmodischen Glamour spiegelt sich
sehr oft in meinen Arbeiten wider."*

*« La peinture me permet de rendre
visuellement accessibles les petites histoires
cinématographiques que j'ai en tête.
Ma passion pour le glamour vintage est
souvent reflétée dans mes créations. »*

↑   Welcome back to Manderley,
2007, personal work; acrylic on canvas

→   Really F....d off!, 2006,
personal work; acrylic on canvas

→→ I-Glam, 2007, personal work;
acrylic on canvas

Sabrina Tibourtine

1979 born in Paris, France | lives and works in Cologne, Germany
www.eine-der-guten.de

EXHIBITIONS

1. "Schöne neue Welt", Bongoût Gallery, Berlin, 2009

2. "Give me one more night", Hug Me Heimlich, Cologne, 2009

3. "FotoGrafik", Galerie Kunstradar, Düsseldorf, 2008

"My work has an imperfect, recycled and used-a-lot look, somehow whimsical and surrealistic at the second glance."

„Meine Arbeiten wirken unvollkommen, recycelt und sehen aus, als wären sie schon oft verwendet worden, auf den zweiten Blick auch irgendwie wunderlich und surrealistisch."

« Mon travail a un aspect imparfait, recyclé et usé, légèrement fantasque et surréaliste en y regardant de plus près. »

↑ Ton pied, le bateau, 2009, University of Siegen, editorial; collage and Adobe Photoshop

→ I know this place, 2011, personal work; collage and Adobe Photoshop

→→ Skip roping doll, 2009, University of Siegen, editorial; collage and Adobe Photoshop

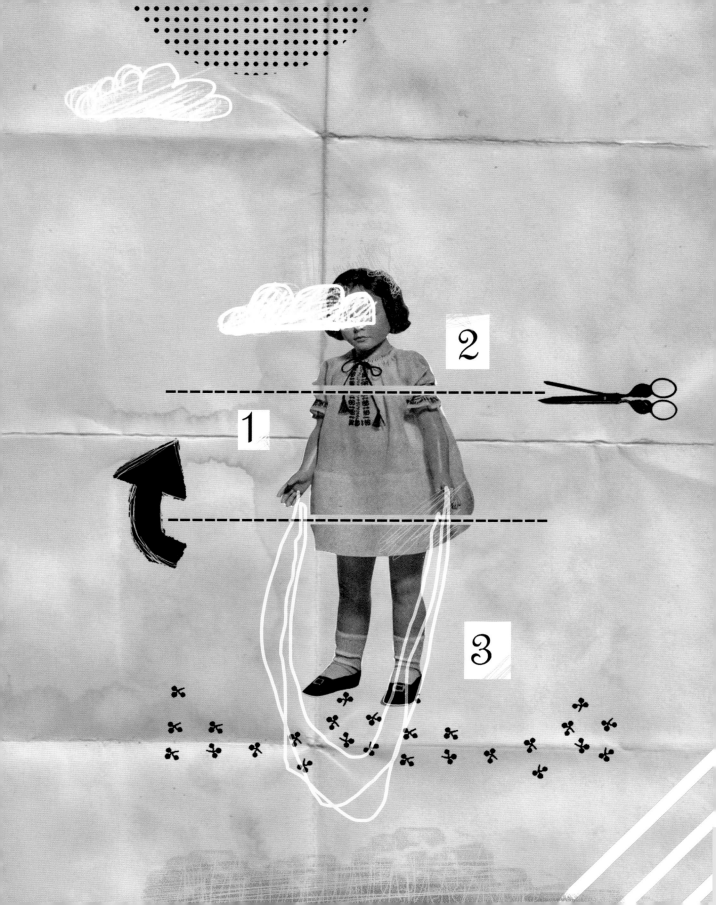

Kaloian Toshev

1986 born in Sofia, Bulgaria | lives and works in Sofia, Bulgaria
www.kaloiantoshev.com

EXHIBITIONS

1. Sofia Architecture
Week, 2009

2. Masters Remastered,
2008

"I create my style by combining the freedom of traditional drawing with the simple shapes of the vector program. I never stop experimenting."

„Ich kreiere meinen Stil, indem ich die Freiheit des traditionellen Zeichnens mit den einfachen Formen eines Vektorprogramms kombiniere. Ich höre nie auf zu experimentieren."

« Je crée mon style en combinant la liberté du dessin traditionnel et les formes simples du vectoriel. J'expérimente tout le temps. »

↑ Dull Life, 2009, personal work; tablet and digital

→ Why am I so young and so bored?, 2010, personal work; tablet and digital

→→ Art is Hard Series, 2008, personal work; tablet and digital

Marco Tóxico

1982 born in La Paz, Bolivia | lives and works in La Paz, Bolivia
www.marcotoxico.com

EXHIBITIONS

1. "Infierno Barroco", Espacio Simón I. Patiño, La Paz, 2011

2. Lápiz, Comunidad Boliviana de Ilustradores, 15º International del Libro, La Paz, 2010

3. International Poster Biennial, Museo San Francisco, La Paz, 2009

4. Dr. Knoche, Museo de la Estampa y del Diseño Carlos Cruz-Diez, Caracas, 2008

5. "Historietas Reales", Centro Cultural Recoleta, Buenos Aires, 2007

↑ Dúo Abrelata, 2011, personal work; Corel Painter

→ Journalists Attacked, 2010, *Parte y Contraparte* magazine; Corel Painter

→→ Gringo Tuerto, 2008, personal work; hand-drawing and Adobe Photoshop

"My artwork is a bad collage of extreme movies, weird Internet sites, bizarre songs and the agoraphobia that you only get living in La Paz City."

„Meine Kunst ist eine schlechte Collage außergewöhnlicher Filme, fremdartiger Internetseiten, bizarrer Songs und jener Platzangst, die man nur bekommt, wenn man in La Paz City lebt."

« Mon œuvre est un mauvais collage de films décalés, de sites Internet étranges, de chansons bizarres et de l'agoraphobie que seule la ville de La Paz est capable de déclencher. »

↑   Invasor "Invader", 2010, personal
work; Corel Painter

←← The Delights of the Tiny Devil, 2011,
Círculo Vicioso, badges; Corel Painter

Thanos Tsilis

1977 born in Athens, Greece | lives and works in Athens, Greece
www.mothica.net

AGENT
Smart Magna
Greece
www.smartmagna.com

"Versatile digital artist, combining animation, games, advertising and book illustrations."

„Vielseitiger digitaler Künstler kombiniert Animation, Spiele, Werbung und Buchillustrationen."

« Artiste numérique versatile, qui combine l'animation, les jeux, la publicité et les illustrations de livres. »

↑   La Bohème, 2010, personal work;
Adobe Photoshop and Corel Painter

→   Christmas Card, 2009, personal work;
Adobe Photoshop and Corel Painter

→→ Cup, 2009, personal work;
Adobe Photoshop

Yury Ustsinau

1979 born in Vitebsk, Belarus | lives and works in Frankfurt am Main, Germany
www.ustsinau.com

"The combination of the two extremes of the colour spectrum: black for absorption of all light, and white for reflection of all light."

„Die Kombination der beiden Extreme des Farbspektrums: Schwarz für die Absorption des gesamten Lichts und Weiß für dessen komplette Reflexion."

« La combinaison des deux extrémités du spectre des couleurs : le noir pour absorber toute la lumière, le blanc pour la réfléchir. »

↑   Buldo, 2010, personal work; plywood, acrylic, hand-drawing

→→ Kosik, 2011, personal work; plywood, acrylic, hand-drawing

Emma Vakarelova

1988 born in Sofia, Bulgaria | lives and works in Sofia, Bulgaria and in Angoulême, France
www.youbook.fr/emmavakarelova

EXHIBITIONS

1. Angoulême's International Festival of Bande Dessinée, 2011

2. CJ Picture Book Award, Seoul, 2010

3. International Humor Exhibition of Piracicaba, 2010

4. "I Heard a Song", Debut Gallery, Sofia, 2006

5. "The Planet Emmaange", solo show, Metropolitan Library, Sofia, 2001

↑ The Snowdrop, 2009, personal work; pastels and pencils

→ Je me defends contre les ennemis invisibles, 2009, personal work; watercolour and gouache

→→ Autumn for Beginners, 2010, personal work; mixed media on canvas

> *"When I paint, I fly over a magic garden, full of secrets, that I can illuminate only with the light of fireflies!"*
>
> *„Wenn ich male, fliege ich über einen magischen Garten voller Geheimnisse, die ich nur mit dem Licht der Glühwürmchen erhellen kann!"*
>
> *« Quand je peins, je survole un jardin magique rempli de secrets, que je peux uniquement éclairer à la lumière des lucioles ! »*

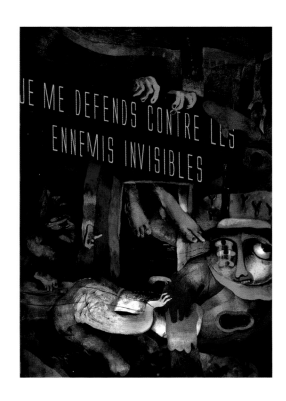

Sam Vanallemeersch

1978 born in Turnhout, Belgium | lives and works in Antwerp, Belgium
www.sovchoz.be

AGENT
Pazuzu
Antwerp
www.pazuzu.be

EXHIBITIONS
1. Atelier Solarshop,
Antwerp

2. Mekanik Strip,
Antwerp

3. S.A.S., Copenhagen

"I don't have a clue, I just want to draw every possible thing I can imagine."

„Ich habe keinen blassen Schimmer, ich will bloß alles Mögliche zeichnen, was ich mir vorstellen kann."

« Je ne sais pas, je veux juste dessiner tout ce que je suis capable d'imaginer. »

↑   The warm-up was a pompous affair, 2010, personal work; hand-drawing

→→   Girls, 2010, personal work; hand-drawing

Brecht Vandenbroucke

1986 born in Veurne, Belgium | lives and works in Ghent, Belgium
http://brechtvandenbroucke.blogspot.com

AGENT
Lezilus
Paris
www.lezilus.com

EXHIBITIONS

1. Fumetto Comic Festival, Luzern, 2011

2. "Anxiety", solo show, Nobrow Gallery, London, 2010

3. "Brecht Vandenbroucke", Delkographic Studio, Rennes, 2010

4. "All Work, No Play", solo show, K&K Gallery, Brussels, 2010

5. "Aller – Retour : rencontres graphiques Paris–Bruxelles", Maison des Metallos, Paris, 2010

"I don't want to express my personal emotions, I want to trigger and evoke them in the heads of other people."

„Ich will keine persönlichen Gefühle ausdrücken, ich will sie in den Köpfen anderer Menschen auslösen und heraufbeschwören."

« Je ne veux pas exprimer mes émotions personnelles, je veux les déclencher et les réveiller chez autrui. »

↑ Antwerp, 2009, Turnleft Guides, poster; acrylic

→ Suspicious, 2010, *Dead* magazine; acrylic

→→ Taxi 1, 2010, *Humo* magazine; acrylic

Mateu Velasco

1980 born in New York (NY), USA | lives and works in Rio de Janeiro (RJ), Brazil
www.mateuvelasco.com

*"My work is about things that we can see
but do not notice. My art tries to show
different meanings of simple things
from our day-by-day experience."*

*„In meiner Arbeit geht es um Dinge, die wir sehen,
aber nicht bemerken. In meiner Kunst versuche ich,
die verschiedenen Bedeutungen einfacher Dinge
aus unserer alltäglichen Erfahrung zu zeigen."*

*«Mon travail porte sur ce que l'on peut voir mais
que l'on ne remarque pas. Mon art tente de révéler
les différentes significations de choses simples
issues du quotidien.»*

↑   Rio, 2011, Design da Gema, website;
Indian ink and digital painting

→→ Octopus City, 2009, IdeaFixa, poster;
Indian ink and digital painting

↑ Oh, really!, 2009, Homegrown support underground, T-shirt; Indian ink and digital painting

→→ Untitled, 2010, Clube do Teatro, poster; Indian ink and digital painting

Susana Villegas

1975 born in La Paz, Bolivia | lives and works in La Paz, Bolivia
www.susanavillegas.deviantart.com

EXHIBITIONS

1. International Comics Festival, La Paz, 2010

2. "Fiesta Pagana", Simón I. Patiño, La Paz, 2008

3. Salón Internacional de Arte, SIART, La Paz, 2003

4. "Observación Agua", Salón de la Academia Nacional de Bellas Artes, Hernando Siles, 2001

↑   Young Stripper, 2010, personal work; Adobe Photoshop

→   Boy, 2010, personal work; Adobe Photoshop

→→ Revenge, 2010, personal work; Adobe Photoshop and Pixologic ZBrush

> *"My work is most influenced by my academic and traditional background. Elements like anatomy, geometry and figure-drawing are always important for me."*
>
> „*Meine Arbeiten werden am meisten von meinem akademischen und traditionellen Hintergrund beeinflusst. Elemente wie Anatomie, Geometrie und Figurenzeichnen sind für mich immer wichtig.*"
>
> « *Mon travail est surtout influencé par mon bagage académique et traditionnel. Des domaines comme l'anatomie, la géométrie et le dessin de modèles ont toujours de l'importance pour moi.* »

Mathew Vincent

1973 born in Providence (RI), USA | lives and works in Lincoln (RI), USA

AGENT
Anna Goodson
Canada
www.agoodson.com

← Carpet, 2009, magazine cover;
pencil and Adobe Photoshop

→→ Hot Spots, 2008, *Scientific American*
magazine; pencil and Adobe Photoshop

*"Portraying a down-to-earth style through
observing the beauty, gesture, interaction,
and design in the global environment."*

*„Einen bodenständigen Stil durch Beobachten
von Schönheit, Gesten, Interaktion und Design
in der globalen Umgebung porträtieren."*

*« Représenter un style pragmatique en observant
la beauté, les gestes, les interactions et
le design dans l'environnement global. »*

↑   Protests, 2010, *Reader's Digest*
magazine (Canada); pencil
and Adobe Photoshop

↘   Freud, 2010, *Harper's* magazine;
pencil and Adobe Photoshop

↑   Reputation, 2007, CCWorldwide;
pencil and Adobe Photoshop

Visca

1980 born in São Paulo (SP), Brazil | lives and works in São Paulo (SP), Brazil
www.viscafactory.com

EXHIBITIONS

1. "Urban Intervention", group show, Paralela Gift Fair, São Paulo, 2011

2. "Among Others", group show, Gallery Soma, São Paulo, 2010

3. "Rojo® Ocho", global group show, Rojo Artspace (Pop), São Paulo, 2009

4. "Electronics Invasion", solo show, Gallery Volcom Flagship, São Paulo, 2008

5. "454 years of São Paulo", group show, Institute of Contemporary Art, 2008

"I like to investigate issues for the individual in the metropolis, the urban and contemporary questions. I love to draw and I love to work with drawing."

„Ich untersuche gerne die Herausforderungen des Individuums in der Metropole, die urbanen und zeitgemäßen Fragen. Ich zeichne für mein Leben gerne und liebe es, mit Zeichnungen zu arbeiten."

« J'aime étudier les questions qui concernent l'individu dans la métropole, des sujets urbains et contemporains. J'aime dessiner et j'aime travailler avec le dessin. »

↑ My Landscapes Series, 2009, Rojo Ocho global group exhibition and book; hand-drawing, Chinese ink and Adobe Photoshop.

→→ The Good Bait, 2009, personal work; hand-drawing, pen nib, Chinese ink, Sumi brush and Adobe Photoshop

Michael Wandelmaier

1979 born in Montreal (QC), Canada | lives and works in Toronto (ON), Canada
www.wandelmaier.com

"The best stories are buried deep in our childhood. I try to dig them up whenever I draw."

„Die besten Storys sind tief in unserer Kindheit vergraben. Beim Zeichnen versuche ich immer, sie auszugraben."

« Les meilleures histoires sont enfouies au plus profond de notre enfance. Je tente de creuser et de les exhumer quand je dessine. »

↑ Krampusnacht, 2010, group show, Resistor Gallery; graphite on Bristol with digital colouring

→ Kangaroo Rat, 2009, The Ark Project, IDN/DGPH; graphite on Bristol with digital colouring

→→ Ruffled Feathers, 2009, personal work; graphite on Bristol with digital colouring

←← Open House Festival, 2011, Random House Canada, poster; graphite on Bristol with digital colouring

→ Squidface & the Meddler, 2010, personal work; graphite on Bristol with digital colouring

↓ Harpooning the Woolly Whale, 2009, personal work; graphite on Bristol with digital colouring

Ben Weeks

1980 born in Toronto (ON), Canada | lives and works in Toronto (ON), Canada
www.benweeks.ca

Let's Draw!

"*Playful, simple, complex, elegant forms, bold graphic line drawings.*"

„*Spielerische, einfache, komplexe, elegante Formen, gewagte grafische Linienzeichnungen.*"

«*Des formes ludiques, simples, complexes, élégantes, des dessins aux lignes audacieuses.*»

↑   Let's Draw!, 2011, Applied Arts;
pen, ink and digital

→→ What is a Sophisticated Investor?,
2010, *Bloomberg Businessweek* magazine;
pen, ink and digital

Alice Wellinger

1962 born in Lustenau, Austria | lives and works in Lustenau, Austria
www.alice-wellinger.com

*"As a matter of fact I am totally
different but rarely get round to it."*

„Ich bin eigentlich ganz anders,
aber ich komme so selten dazu."

« En fait je suis complètement différent,
mais je le comprends rarement. »

— Ödön von Horvath

↑ Locked in, 2010,
personal work; acrylic

→ Medicine from the rainforest,
2010, *Vital* magazine; acrylic
and Adobe Photoshop

→→ My life as a mandrill, 2010,
personal work; acrylic and
Adobe Photoshop

↑ Kurt bends bananas, 2010,
personal work; acrylic and
Adobe Photoshop

↓ Confession: "I can't stop talking
nonsense" and Confession: "What was the
Question?" 2011, personal work; acrylic

↑ The flight of the oppressed,
2011, *Gööo* magazine; acrylic
and Adobe Photoshop

→ Adolf as a child, 2010,
personal work; acrylic

Stephanie Wunderlich

1966 born in Munich, Germany | lives and works in Hamburg, Germany
www.wunderlich-illustration.de

AGENT
Threeinabox
Toronto
www.threeinabox.net

EXHIBITIONS
1. "Das Magazin und seine Illustratoren", Neurotitan Gallery, Berlin, 2011

2. "In 50 Comics um die Welt", Neurotitan Gallery, Berlin, 2010

3. Spring Release, Hinterconi Gallery, Hamburg, 2010

4. Spring Release, Gallery Neurotitan, Berlin, 2009

5. "Auf allen Vieren", Westwerk, Hamburg, 1999

"I love making collage illustration using a graphic, striking and reduced style."

„Ich liebe es, Illustrationen aus Collagen zu schaffen und dabei einen grafischen, auffälligen und reduzierten Stil zu verwenden."

« J'aime faire des illustrations en collage avec un style graphique restreint et frappant. »

↑ Look at yourself, 2011, personal work; collage

→ Avatar, 2009, personal work; collage

→→ Nutrition in autumn, 2008, *Freundin* magazine; collage

Yuji Yamada

1985 born in Kamakura, Japan | lives and works in Kawasaki, Japan
www.yamada.mods.jp

"I find beauty in sports photos."

„Ich finde Sportfotos unwahrscheinlich schön."

« Je trouve de la beauté dans les photos sportives. »

↑ Nobeyama CX #3, 2010, personal work; acrylic

→→ Shoulder, 2010, personal work; acrylic

Olimpia Zagnoli

1984 born in Reggio Emilia, Italy | lives and works in Milan, Italy and in New York (NY), USA
www.olimpiazagnoli.com

AGENT 1
Marlena Agency
Princeton
www.marlenaagency.com

AGENT 2
Illustrissimo
Paris
www.illustrissimo.com

EXHIBITIONS
1. Adidas Originals,
solo show, Vice Gallery,
Milan, 2009

2. "Spread the lead",
Gallery Hanahou,
New York, 2008

"I like to work with graphical and clean illustrations with a retro feel. I like to play with shapes and lines and make them do a little dance before creating the final piece. My inspiration comes from the great artists of the past mixed with psychedelic night visions and some pop songs."

„Ich arbeite gerne mit grafischen und klaren Illustrationen mit einem Retro-Touch. Dann spiele ich gerne mit Formen und Linien und lasse sie für mich ein wenig tanzen, bevor ich das Werk endgültig abschließe. Ich lasse mich von den großen Künstlern der Vergangenheit inspirieren, gemischt mit psychedelischen nächtlichen Visionen und einigen Popsongs."

«J'aime travailler avec des illustrations graphiques et épurées de style rétro. J'aime jouer avec les formes et les lignes et les faire danser un peu avant de finaliser mon œuvre. Mon inspiration vient des grands artistes du passé et de visions nocturnes psychédéliques, ainsi que de certaines chansons pop.»

↑ Protecting our Children, 2011, Internazionale; Adobe Illustrator

→→ Harmony, 2011, *Vice* magazine; Adobe Illustrator

Zenk One

1981 born in Tilburg, Netherlands | lives and works in Breda, Netherlands
www.zenkone.nl

AGENT
Shop Around
Netherlands
www.shop-around.nl

EXHIBITIONS

1. GreyTones, Bomhuis Breda, 2010

2. An Artist collection, Kingdom Tilburg, 2010

3. Graphic Design Festival 2010, Breda

4. Alias, Bomhuis Breda, 2006

5. Vogelvrij Gallery, Roermond, 2006

"I love to draw, love to paint, love to build."

„Ich liebe das Zeichnen, ich liebe das Malen, ich liebe das Bauen."

«J'aime dessiner, peindre et construire.»

↑   Untitled, 2010, Rugby Division, poster, advertising, website, T-shirt, Art Direction: Jurgen van Zachten; hand-drawing and Adobe Illustrator

→   Untitled, 2009, Landgut Strumpffabrik (Germany), wall painting; hand-drawing and Adobe Illustrator

→→ Great Buffalo Head Spirit, 2010, Misterthree, T-shirt; hand-drawing and Adobe Illustrator

Kareena Zerefos

1983 born in Sydney, Australia | lives and works in London, United Kingdom
www.kareenazerefos.com

EXHIBITIONS

1. Contempo, Libby Edwards Galleries, Melbourne, 2010

2. The Happy Tree, Monster Children Gallery, Sydney, 2010

3. United Galleries Hip Hop, Saatchi & Saatchi Sydney, 2009

4. Hand Drawn, Nine Lives Gallery, Brisbane, 2009

5. MTV Gallery, solo show, Sydney, 2008

"I have an unhealthy obsession with dangerously sharp 2B pencils, which may or may not be associated with my perfectionist Virgo tendencies… and my pencils, along with a yearning to escape to a world of make-believe, lead me to create whimsical illustrative work with a sense of isolation and bitter-sweet nostalgia."

„Ich habe eine ungesunde Neigung zu gefährlich spitzen 2B-Bleistiften, was vielleicht mit meinem Hang zur Perfektion als Jungfrau zu tun hat… oder auch nicht… und neben meinem Verlangen, in eine Welt der Fantasie zu flüchten, verleiten meine Stifte mich dazu, ein skurriles illustratives Werk mit einem Hauch Isolation und bittersüßer Nostalgie zu kreieren.“

« J'ai une obsession maladive pour les crayons 2B dangereusement pointus, peut-être liée à mes tendances perfectionnistes de native de la Vierge. Mes crayons, ainsi que mon envie de m'échapper dans un monde imaginaire, me poussent à créer des œuvres illustratives fantasques avec un sentiment d'isolement et de nostalgie douce-amère. »

↑ Runaway Girl, 2011, *Cent* magazine; hand-drawing, graphite, ink and Copic markers on paper

→→ From the Menagerie, 2011, personal work; hand-drawing, graphite and ink on paper

↑ Flying Owl, 2010, Element Eden;
hand-drawing, ink, pencil and
Copic markers

←← Carnival Horses, 2008, personal work;
hand-drawing, graphite, ink, gouache
and Adobe Illustrator

Acknowledgements / Danksagungen / Remerciements

First and foremost, my sincere thanks go to all the illustrators for supplying the most astonishing work and for constantly keeping in touch with us in order to improve the end result. My other big thanks, of course, go to Daniel Siciliano Bretas, my right hand at TASCHEN headquarters in Cologne. Daniel worked tirelessly on the design and layout, paying meticulous attention to detail and delivering the final proofs in record time. I would also like to express my sincere gratitude to Steven Heller, who worked closely with us to select a truly diverse showcase of creative talent, as well as Bruno Porto, who is based in Shanghai but contributed hugely with ideas and a really bright essay on how illustrators work today. Their expertise was of the greatest importance for this publication, and their vast knowledge of illustration is unsurpassed. On our production front, Stefan Klatte has done an amazing job from beginning to end, and through his valiant efforts we were, as always, able to optimise each step of the production process, improving the quality along the way. I would also like to acknowledge all the illustrators' agents, who were always on hand to lend us their support, and all the friends and illustrators that voluntarily keep sending us great recommendations for the next publication.

Julius Wiedemann

← Untitled, by Mateu Velasco,
2010, personal work; ink and digital

Imprint

© 2011 TASCHEN GmbH
Hohenzollernring 53, D-50672 Köln
www.taschen.com

To stay informed about upcoming TASCHEN titles,
please request our magazine at www.taschen.com/magazine
or write to TASCHEN, Hohenzollernring 53, D-50672 Cologne,
Germany, contact@taschen.com, Fax: +49-221-254919.
We will be happy to send you a free copy of our magazine
which is filled with information about all of our books.

Design and layout: Daniel Siciliano Bretas
Production: Stefan Klatte

Editor: Julius Wiedemann
Editorial Coordination: Daniel Siciliano Bretas

English Revision: Chris Allen
German Translation: Jürgen Dubau
French Translation: Valérie Lavoyer for Equipo de Edición

Printed in Italy
ISBN 978–3–8365–2423–0